MW00874724

The Art of Attracting Authentic LOVE

A Transformational Four-Step Process

Gayla Wick

BALBOA. PRESS
A DIVISION OF HAY HOUSE

Balboa Press books may be ordered through booksellers or by contacting:

Balboa Press
A Division of Hay House
1663 Liberty Drive
Bloomington, IN 47403
www.balboapress.com
1 (877) 407-4847

Print information available on the last page.

ISBN: 978-1-5043-4654-2 (sc)
ISBN: 978-1-5043-4656-6 (hc)
ISBN: 978-1-5043-4655-9 (e)

Library of Congress Control Number: 2015919798

Balboa Press rev. date: 01/15/2016

Dedication

This book is dedicated to ***Allan Wick***, my husband, best friend, and love of my life. I am eternally grateful for our relationship and to the ***Universe*** for orchestrating our first kiss.

Your love and support enriches my life every day.

Table of Contents

Part III: Fact or Fiction?

Acknowledgements

This book would not have been possible without the courageous women who so willingly gave their time, wisdom, (and sometimes their tears) by sharing their most personal of stories. May your unique love partnerships grow richer every day. Thank you for your inspirational stories!

Enormous gratitude goes to my fabulous and exacting editor, ***Betty Ridolfi***. Thank you so much for your contribution to my work and for the "cookies" you so generously left throughout my manuscript!!

Thank you to my parents, ***JR*** and ***Dorothy,*** for providing unconditional love, a nurturing environment throughout my life, and for teaching me that with *Spirit* all things are possible.

To my beautiful and compassionate daughter, ***Alexandra;*** and to my strong and generous son, ***Joshua***: I wish for both of you the pure and genuine love of a true partnership that enriches your lives as you desire. Your love for me - even when I embarrass you – means more than I can say.

Thank you to Donna and Lisa, the best two sisters anyone could ever wish for. Being there with me through the darkness and the light has always made such a difference in my life. I love you dearly.

To my brother, ***Joe***: My love for you is eternal.

I feel deep gratitude for all of my ***friends*** (too numerous to list) for believing in me. Your encouragement helped to make it possible for me to leave my corporate career, step into a new life, write a book, and become a Transformational Love Coach! For all of that, I am eternally grateful!

Preface

I used to think "true romance," finding the "love of my life" and living happily ever after, was far worse than a simple fairy tale. I thought a few hopeless romantics or liars made up that thought just to make the rest of us roll our eyes and want to be sick. I believed that sentiment through most of my young adulthood, while the life I wanted slowly eroded like sand on the beach. I decided that the old saying, "Relationships are hard work" must be how it really is and I berated myself for wanting anything different in the first place.

Just like my parents and their parents, I married the man I loved, and I planned to stay married until "death do us part." It took a very long time for me to understand a comment made by one of my friends. She said, "There are many ways for a marriage or relationship to die." Hearing this gave me a very different perspective. I'd always thought "until death do us part" meant exactly what it said - someone was in a coffin.

I wrote this book because I – (like so many others I know) – have suffered unfulfilling relationships and struggled to know what to think or to do about our situations. I was married for over twenty years and spent many, if not most, of those years seeking something I could not name or find. Mostly, I thought I needed to try harder, change the way I was feeling, and simply accept the fact that "Marriages are hard work."

That idea never fully resonated with me. I did not understand how something that was supposed to be fulfilling and pleasurable could actually end up being such hard work every day. That level of effort on a daily basis didn't seem to be what I really wanted in a relationship after a long and tiring day at work. I realized it was so exhausting, attempting to keep an intimate relationship solid, growing, and headed in a mutually agreed upon direction.

When my relationship ended, the relief I felt was all I wanted, relief and perhaps a little peace from the incessant demands of my marriage. Happiness seemed far too lofty a goal. The constant hard work had left me feeling drained and over-all pretty pessimistic about enjoying mutually satisfying love. After some time alone, reading great books, and meeting new friends, I recovered my sense of self and found my own measure of happiness. It was a choice I made quite consciously: to be happy in the circumstances in which I found myself. Now, in my mid-forties, I was soon to be an officially divorced woman with two teenage children. Having lost my house, I was living in an apartment; and, in many ways, I was starting over to rebuild my life. However, I was totally blindsided by what happened next.

Much to my surprise, the partner of my dreams walked into my life. Then I knew what I'd been missing – true intimacy. Our love relationship was soul-satisfying; something far more pleasurable than I'd ever hoped for. It felt almost too good to be true, but it was genuine, real beyond any dream, thought or expectation I'd ever had. Before you sigh or roll your eyes, please know I'm not talking about morning, noon and night ecstasy. I'm describing a balance tipped significantly to the side of easy flowing pleasure – a sanctuary for the heart.

This book is about finding that kind of true intimacy – the missing piece I could not name until it came to me so surprising and sweet, wrapped and then unwrapped like a special birthday present. It happened when I least expected it, when I wasn't even consciously looking. I hadn't dared to imagine I could have the romantic satisfying relationship many women dream of and often see so vividly portrayed in the movies. Now I know it's real and I understand much more about how it happens.

I want each one of you to have the love relationship of your dreams - that is, if you want it. I truly believe this is possible and it can definitely happen. You can have a partner that shares your life in all those large and small ways that bring joy, happiness, and soul-satisfying pleasure to your daily life.

Before writing about how I thought this process works, I decided to conduct research by interviewing other women who'd found the love of their lives. I talked with women from across the country, and I will share several of their stories with you. I found them to be quite instructive and inspiring, and I hope you will benefit from them as I have. Most of all, I wish for you the long lasting, soul-satisfying love you've always desired. If you are already in this kind of relationship, then you are truly blessed.

However, if you are still searching for your love connection, I hope you are curious enough not only to read on and accept my invitation to consider what I am going to share with you but also perhaps to try it out for yourself.

Introduction

Why don't I have the love of my life and the love relationship of my dreams? Why am I still single after all the things I've done to find my love connection? What's the real secret to having my heart's desire? Why do I seem to attract all the wrong types of men?

If you've been asking any of these types of questions, you're not alone. I've written this book especially for you. You deserve clear answers, but not from just anyone. If you want to hear from someone who's been where you are – disappointed in love, and then discovered how finding love really works - then you're in the right place.

This book was written to provide you with clear answers in an easy to follow step-by- step *Love Coaching Plan*. I'll explain how the three parts of the book work together to give you a roadmap forward. No more detours or roadblocks for you. You may want to read the book through once before starting the *Love Coaching Program* exercises or you may consider each chapter's advice and apply it before moving forward. You should do whatever you decide works best for you.

The book begins with *My Story* because I want you to feel reassured that you are not alone in being deeply disappointed by your previous experiences with love and/or marriage. Most people enter into intimate relationships with their highest intentions as I did. However, as experience demonstrates, intentions cannot stand alone. I was raised to believe divorce was not only the ultimate personal failure, but a sin ranking right up there alongside high treason. Imagine the implications of that belief on a young woman as she faced emotional battery, financial and spiritual abandonment, and fear of raising two small children alone.

Regardless of your personal love relationship history, you can rise above it and attract the love of your life. If you are willing to consider another way, I'm here to guide you. In order for this Love Coaching Program to work, you certainly don't have to believe any particular philosophy or engage in any activities in which you'd rather not participate. I only ask that you be willing to say goodbye to things that haven't worked and embrace a willingness to try something new; set aside any disbelief in the possibility of attracting the love of your life.

Since you're reading this book, I'm sure you're tired of trying to figure everything out by yourself. You're frustrated over how many relationships haven't worked out the way you thought they would, or you're feeling depleted by searching for love and coming up with nothing. It does not need to be this way any longer. By opening this book you have the option to embark on a new path. So breathe, relax, and begin knowing you are ready to accelerate the process of finding your love connection.

Family and friends may not be so enthusiastic about your new plan. They most likely mean well, but they haven't been walking in your shoes. If they had great love relationship advice, I'm sure you know what it is by now. Only you know how many activities you've put your body, mind and spirit into while attempting to find love. Now you are doing something for yourself – engaging in a new way of thinking about and attracting love. Beware of skeptics and naysayers. Right now you need a cheerleader, mentor, and coach. My plan is to explain everything and give you a clear step-by-step guide to follow.

What's in the Book?

The book is divided into three parts, each with easy to follow exercises.

Part I: Creating the Foundation - I talk about key building blocks required for creating a sustainable long-term love relationship. There are chapters on character, intimacy, trust, authenticity, and gratitude. Each chapter has a story or two from women just like you that illustrates the main points. Following the story, each chapter concludes with questions for group discussion and self-reflection. Regardless of whether you are reading alone or in a group, you'll want to take time to consider each question and give yourself enough time to thoughtfully answer.

The ***Love Coaching Program*** begins in **Part II: It's All About You**. There are four chapters in this section, along with more illustrative stories following each chapter. This is the part of the book which outlines in detail the process for shifting your energy and focus from what you don't have to the infinite possibilities. To support you on this new path, I've included a variety of exercises for each of the four steps. Again, you can follow this program yourself or in a group setting. You'll be led on a step-by-step journey which you'll hopefully enjoy while making a significant transition in your love attraction story. Be sure to relax and take your time with this program. Stress and tension will not positively contribute to your goals. This program was designed to create optimal success with minimal struggle and angst.

Part III: Fact or Fiction - There are four chapters: *Relationship Myths, Relationship Realities, Conclusion,* and *The Research.* Each of the chapters has one or more enlightening stories as well. I want you to know more about some of the most common myths we've all heard about love and marriage and why they are untrue. Of course, once you know the advice you've been given that's fiction, I want you to know the facts – or as I call them, *Relationship Realities.* This information will help you create the authentic truly intimate love relationship you desire.

The Research chapter includes the results of the yearlong research project I conducted while writing this book. I interviewed happily coupled women from across the country to find out just how they attracted the love relationship of their dreams. I was astonished to discover the common themes in their stories. I loved learning more about how attracting love really works, and I decided to share the results with all the single women reading this book who desire their own love connection. You'll read my story and many others throughout the book. I hope you are inspired to follow this *Love Coaching Program* to attract the love relationship of your dreams.

Chapter One

My Story

I thought I was going to die. The wide dirt road near our house where I often walked was once again the scene of my despair. There I collapsed in the middle of it crying as I'd done many times before. If the prolific skunk population in our semi-rural setting didn't get me, a car would probably run me over.

I'd had enough and felt like I couldn't go another day not knowing what to do. Angry and hurt, I felt so alone with a load of family responsibilities and no help from my partner. I asked *Spirit* to send someone to help me, anyone who would actually know what to do. My need to figure it out myself went out the window. I left the "how" to *Universal Creative Mind.* Certainly, a power that created all there is can and would guide me out of the darkness.

It had been too much – the job, the kids, the house, the yard, the bills, the cars, and the husband acting like another child instead of the partner he promised to be. The situation I'd always thought was temporary morphed day-by-day into months and years. It wasn't going to improve. It would only get worse. Our private conflicts became more public as he began to raise his voice, belittling me loudly enough for others to hear. The emotional battering left me confused and unsure of what to do. At times I wished he would physically hit me so I would know for sure it was time to leave.

I'd meant every word I said on our wedding day in the lovely white historic chapel surrounded by beautiful hand laid stone walls. The horse drawn carriage driven by the elderly gentleman wearing his black top hat carried me to the front door. My hopes were high for a long and blissful union.

Like most weddings, not everything was perfect. The wedding cake was late and no one expected the light drizzle of rain. However, the real gorilla in the room was his parents – awkwardly absent. Apparently a young woman from a family of modest means pursuing an education and a career was not good enough for their only child. In spite of his pleas, they refused our wedding invitation. I was young and lacked the good sense to know this was more than a bad beginning. His family had rejected me from the start. The fact that we'd dated for nearly five years and loved each other seemed to have no effect on them.

We'd been raised in similar environments, I from West Virginia and he from Ohio. Our faith traditions were the same – both regularly attending a conservative fundamentalist church with the same name over the door. He was in graduate school when we met; I was in a graduate degree program, planning a career in law enforcement or private security.

On one of our rare visits, his mother said, "Career women neglect their husbands." I thought that was completely absurd. Having watched our family struggle periodically on one income, I'd planned since junior high school to pursue an education and have my own source of income. No amount of dialogue or common sense changed his parents' minds. But we were in love and went ahead with our wedding as planned.

For many years, I was happy. We had a beautiful healthy daughter, followed twenty-one months later by a healthy adorable son. Actually, when I first saw my son, he looked a bit like a wrinkly red faced old man. I wanted to say, "Oh my beautiful baby," but that wasn't true just yet. He quickly evolved into a darling cherub-faced little brother.

The speed of life accelerated with the arrival of children. The faster it went, the more I did and the less he contributed. Where and when the fork in the road occurred, I really don't know. I just know that he went one way and I went another.

That night in the middle of the road, I felt something shift. Something viscerally changed as I pulled myself from the dirt, dusted myself off, wiped my tears, and headed home. I knew on the deepest level that I'd been heard.

Months passed and nothing changed. "How" raged in my brain frequently. Every time I walked into the bathroom, I heard over and over the lines, "The land of the free and the home of the brave" playing loudly in my head. I thought I was losing my mind. What was going on and what did it mean? I intuitively knew what it meant, but divorce was not an option in our family. I was sure I'd go straight to hell.

Hell or not, I could not go on pretending to be the cheerful wife and mother, relaxed and content. In truth I was exhausted and lonely. Our marriage had been over for a long time. The resuscitation efforts were useless. Finally, I accepted what I'd tried so long and hard to avoid – our broken relationship was unrepairable.

Friends were not surprised by my decision to divorce as they had witnessed much of my misery. My parents handled it with more grace than I'd ever imagined, given their strong religious views on marriage. I'd always been close to my two sisters who were wonderfully supportive. After an interminably long and arduous battle with attorneys and court appearances, I was free. Now I had to be brave.

As I began to breathe again, I was able to step out of the daily chaos and endless mind chatter and into peace and relaxation. Fatigue and frustration had turned me into someone I didn't recognize or like. I'd thought about being single a million times. Here I was. It wasn't so bad. I invited tranquility, gratitude, joy, peace, and kindness into my new life. I read any book I wanted to read. No one could ever suddenly move them out of reach again.

I'd made several life changing decisions in the year before leaving my marriage. First, I decided to be happy. That decision changed everything. It didn't happen overnight. Like most changes, it was a work in progress. At times, that decision challenged me to hold onto it, and I did, one moment at a time. When I slipped, I chose not to berate myself. I simply and gently reminded myself to embrace joy rather than fear. Ultimately, I remembered my father's repeated Biblical wisdom that *God* had not given us a spirit of fear.

Allan and I were introduced by a mutual friend while attending a professional association conference. As volunteer leaders for this same organization, we had most likely been in several of the same meetings years earlier. We didn't recall ever seeing each other. He first noticed me on Sunday afternoon when I was giving a lecture on a paper I'd written about the value of membership in this international association. He'd been to this particular training session many times, choosing to chat with a colleague just outside the door. Busy with my presentation, I took no notice of him that day.

On Monday, I attended an educational session where I was scheduled to moderate a panel of three speakers. Allan was one of the panelists, as was my best friend, Bonnie, who'd introduced us. My only thoughts were on the moderator duties, which included individual introductions. I stayed for the remainder of the session and promptly left with Bonnie for an afternoon break.

The following evening, as I mingled with friends at a cocktail party, I saw Allan again. There were dozens of vendor parties that night, all in different locations throughout the city. Since it was common practice to move from party to party for thousands of conference attendees, it was quite unusual for us to be in the same place at the same time. A group of us chatted for a while over food and drinks before going our separate ways. Allan seemed like a very nice man, but romance was far from my mind. I left with my friends and he did likewise.

I particularly loved Wednesday evenings, the annual black tie gala event. I saw him across the room in a tuxedo, a glass of champagne in hand just as I arrived. He said hello, we chatted for several minutes; and as I was leaving to join my friends, he whispered, "You look hot in that dress." Wow – an unexpected compliment from a business colleague I barely knew. I smiled and said thank you, taking my leave; but his comment stayed with me all evening. It had been a long time since I'd received such a glowing compliment.

The ballroom was set with tables for hundreds of people. As I walked through the crowd to find my reserved place, I saw that Allan was at the adjacent table. We were seated very close, backs to each other; and throughout the evening I felt the warmth of his energy. I'd never had such an experience. Later Allan shared he'd had the same experience – feeling my energy as well.

As was customary, volunteer leaders and guests were invited to the Association's Presidential suite after the activity filled day, for cocktails and socializing. Allan was there when I arrived. Fourth time in a row we'd been in the same place. As usual, we had a great time talking with our friends and colleagues. A short time later, our small group, including Allan, decided to go out in the city one last time before returning home. We didn't stay long in the piano bar; it was noisy and the music wasn't the best that night.

Shortly after arriving at a new club, I suddenly became aware that Allan was dancing with my friend. I couldn't understand why that annoyed me so much. Eventually he asked me to dance. There were so many people on the dance floor we had to weave our way through the crowd to find space.

We'd been dancing for less than two minutes when he pulled me close and kissed me. Everyone around us disappeared as I literally felt transported to another world. It was a magical moment – the kind of moment you read about and think is only fantasy. I thought that too, until it happened to me. Allan had the same experience. Later, he told me he'd never been so forward in his life. He had no idea what force had overtaken him. All he remembered was the overwhelming message to kiss me. Our lives were never the same.

He asked me to marry him seventy-five days later. I said yes without a nanosecond of hesitation. There were a trillion miles between us. He lived in Aruba and I in Utah. We fell in love over the phone, talking for hours each day and night. Two days after returning home from the conference where we met, he sent a dozen multi-colored roses, followed by the complete collection of books written by his favorite author, Og Mandino.

The intimacy that developed between us was undeniable. We could not explain the rapid connection because neither intended to ever remarry. Our romance, so surprising and sweet, was meant to be. Years earlier, we'd been in the same room, but did not see each other. Someone or something switched on the light when the time was right. Had we met sooner, neither of us would have been ready.

I don't think I'd ever felt as serene as I did on our wedding day. We were married outside in the courtyard of a Tuscan restaurant under a tent with family and friends. Words seem inadequate to convey the gratitude we feel for our relationship every day. I am cherished and adored and loved unconditionally – as is he. There are no crazy games or hidden agendas, no jealousies or efforts to control. As Ina Garten said, we just want each other to be happy. We don't agree on everything and that's okay because we know how to disagree. We love to be together and make life decisions as a team. The compatibility we share invites harmony, peace, joy, trust, and love. I didn't know any of that was possible before meeting Allan.

My relationship with Allan gave birth to this book. I share it with you to use as you see fit. My fondest wish is for every person to have the love they desire, in their own way, in their own time. My intent is to create a visible pathway to love for those who seek it. I invite you to take what feels right for you and leave the rest.

If you are married or in a long-term committed partnership, I hope you read this book looking for ideas to strengthen your love connection, rather than as a way to measure your relationship. If you are not happy, sit down with your mate and talk about what you had together – what connected and drew you both together from the beginning. See if there's a way to get back anything you are missing. If you need guidance, find a marriage counselor or other support services as needed.

This book is from my heart based on my experiences and those of the many extraordinary women you'll meet in these pages. I hope you enjoy it!

Part I

Creating the Foundation

Chapter Two

Character

You may be asking what character has to do with intimacy. I wondered about their connection as well. As I let the idea float around in my mind and heart, I began to see they are inextricably linked – like hot fudge and ice cream or bread and cheese for a grilled cheese sandwich. Without ice cream to support hot fudge, there would be no delicious hot fudge sundae. Without bread to support the cheese, there would be no scrumptious grilled cheese sandwich. For me, character and intimacy are linked in the same way. Without character supporting intimacy, true intimacy cannot exist.

So what is character? According to dictionary.com, character is defined as, "The aggregate of features and traits that form the individual nature of some person or thing; moral or ethical quality; main or essential nature." When I use the word character in the context of relationship, it is that "essential nature" aspect I find compelling. It is the ability to show-up authentically – spiritually, physically, emotionally, and intellectually as your highest and best self.

Deceit, dishonesty, desire to control another, all undermine the character of true intimacy. However, we must first be authentic, trustworthy, and happy for ourselves before we can treat another person the same way. Attempting to build authentic love relationships requires true character. Desiring absolute trust from a partner requires reciprocity of that trustworthiness. For example, unhappy people simply don't possess peace and happiness to share with someone else. Pretending to be someone other than who we are cannot create the complement of character and intimacy.

Our individual character is developed from the depth and breadth of our experiences and beliefs. Because it is personal, we always own the character we have. Consequently, we're the only ones that can evolve and change the nature of our character. Throughout our lives we learn from others. When we see the need for change or adjustment, we can make the choice to improve whatever it is that needs to improve in our lives. Parents, friends, teachers, books, etc. all model examples of character. If we're aware of our character and its inherent defects, we can choose to modify or change. Changing our character cannot be forced. Lasting change occurs only when we genuinely desire, accept, and make a concentrated effort to create a different character.

If we could fully accept that we cannot change anyone else, we'd be spared so much pain, disappointment, and frustration. The idea that we cannot change another person sounds obvious and fairly straightforward. Most of us can nod our agreement and think we know and readily accept this wisdom. The reality is something altogether different. Can you honestly say you haven't tried to change one of your boyfriends, partners, or husbands? How successful were you? We may think we're going to be the exception and show up in relationships in a way that brings our desired result. However, the failure rate of this endeavor is enormous.

We may be able to talk our partners into trying new things, dressing a little better, or even becoming compliant on a number of things that make our lives with them more pleasant. But if we think we can convince them to change more serious matters of their character, we're on a fool's errand. Whenever others are dishonest with themselves, sooner or later they'll be dishonest with you. If the man you're with is rude and doesn't consider the feelings of others, even if he's on his best behavior with you, sooner or later his true character will shine through and you're at risk of having your feelings trampled.

The essential nature of all people is reflected clearly in their actions. When there is disconnection between words and actions, it's time to consider the truth. If a man says he loves you, ask yourself, "Are his actions supporting his words?"

What is the essential nature of the person with whom you want to spend your life? What is your essential nature? Are you willing to be the person you're looking for? If you want someone who has the characteristics of honesty, integrity, respect, compassion, diligence, financial prudence, loyalty, kindness, generosity, warmth, trustworthiness, patience, affection, etc., you have to be willing to demonstrate those qualities in your life. While this doesn't mean you have to be perfect, it does require clarity around your personal qualities and characteristics, those things you bring to an intimate relationship. Take time to think about your values and how they fit with the kind of partner you want in your life. Starting a relationship with someone who doesn't have the core values or characteristics you have and want can be doomed from day one.

The choice is yours, as well is mine. Although simple and obvious, how many times have you seen yourself or others forget they have a choice? When we remember we have a choice, it doesn't necessarily make the choice easy; it simply makes it possible. For example, if you're in an abusive relationship, remembering you're at a choice point takes the responsibility away from the abuser and empowers you to choose. You can continue taking the abuse or stand up for yourself and move on to a better life.

There was a time when I thought I had no way out of the prison I felt locked into. Because I believed that, I was stuck and unhappy. When I decided to take responsibility for my own well-being, I saw the choice was mine and always had been, even when I did not see it. It's empowering to own our choices, good and bad, and to fully accept that role in our lives.

The next two stories beautifully emphasize this point. The first is about a young woman who knew this instinctively at a very young age. While Marissa was very much in love with her boyfriend, she knew what behaviors were acceptable and what were not for their romance to continue and grow. She also knew that trying to change him wouldn't work. He would need to come to his own understanding and willingly change his behavior. In the meantime, she did not have to settle for anything less than the standards she'd set for herself and her love relationship. This story reveals the forgivable mistakes of youth and illustrates that acceptable character in an intimate relationship is non-negotiable.

"When you grow up and start making choices on what you know to be right, then we can have a relationship."

Marissa

Marissa's Story

When she was still in high school, Marissa told her girlfriend she wished someone who had a cute son would move in next door. When her father, the builder, completed the house on the adjoining lot, that's just what happened. The new neighbors had a son her age. When Marissa saw him from her window, she thought he was indeed the cute boy she'd wished for.

They lived in the Midwest where dust storms were common. Shortly after the new family with the adorable son moved in, the news warned that a dust storm was on its way. Marissa's mother, seeing the car in the neighbor's driveway with the headlights on, instructed Marissa, "Before the storm gets here, go next door and tell the neighbor they've left their car lights on." Marissa didn't want to go. She thought the boy would think she was interested in him. Since her mother insisted, Marissa followed her instructions. Sometime later, Marissa pointed him out to her girlfriend from a distance and said, "See that boy over there – he's going to ask me out."

Don went to a different school, so they didn't see each other every day. Yet, when Marissa noticed him at a social event for multiple schools, within a week, he'd asked her out for sodas at a local drive-in. They dated throughout their senior year of high school and attended prom together. After graduation, Don left for technical school, and the relationship went through some tough times. There were break-ups and make-ups; but when Marissa realized Don needed time to mature, she ended their relationship. Since she was in college preparing for her future, she didn't want to prolong the break-up make-up cycle. She loved him and knew the connection was there from the first time they looked into each other's eyes. If this relationship was meant to be, it would develop when the time was right.

They reunited at the end of Marissa's college junior year and became engaged during her senior year. The boy with the amazing eyes had matured. They were married a few weeks after her graduation and moved away from both their families. Marissa told me they learned to work things out and become a team, even though they were young. She wasn't nervous at the wedding. The feeling she had about this relationship was very clear from the beginning. Though not logical, she knew they were always going to be together. That was twenty-six years ago. She still describes him as the love of her life.

Not being nervous at the wedding is an important point. This seemed to be a common occurrence for the many women I interviewed. They felt a sense of calm at their weddings. They obviously were excited to be marrying their true love, but not nervous because it was so right. No little voices in their heads created panic or chaotic thoughts. When your whole being knows the decision is the right one, a deep feeling of internal peace flows through every cell. This happened to me as well when I remarried.

In the midst of all the chaos before my wedding ceremony: hair and make-up touch-ups; small dressing space with sisters, mother, daughter, maid of honor - all primping and talking photographer coming in and out; excitement filled the air. But the sense of calm I felt was extraordinary.

When all of your being knows the decision you've made is right, there isn't anything to be nervous about; excited yes, but not nervous. If you have wedding plans and you're questioning your decision in any way, if you're feeling panicky or have a sense of impending dread, you might want to stop and reassess what this is about. If you're wondering if you're doing the right thing, the answer is probably no.

Although Marissa was quite young when she met Don, she showed judgment beyond her years to break off the relationship when it did not feel right. When I asked her how she was able to do this at such a young age, she attributed her strength and self-esteem to her father's colorful, but wise, guidance. He'd always told Marissa and her sister, "You don't have to take sh… from anybody, and I want you to remember that."

So many women don't say no when they should. Instead, they accept what is really unacceptable behavior from their partners, even when their internal voices are flashing red flags of warning. Marissa was indeed fortunate to have such a wise father and wiser still to accept his advice and apply it when needed.

This next story comes from a lovely, talented, incredibly smart and compassionate woman who forgot for a while she had choices. Sometimes we need someone to remind and support us in reawakening to our choices. This story illustrates the consequences of giving our choices away in the name of love. I hope you'll feel inspired as I did by Rachel's journey on her path to realizing the power of standing in the truth of her character.

"I'm with you because I choose to be. If you're gone tomorrow, I'll be sad, but I'll be fine because I love me more than I love you."

Rachel

Rachel's Story

When Rachel thought about the type of person she would marry, she had a vision of a man in a suit and tie with a good sense of humor. When she found him, he had the added bonus of being smart. In fact, he had a genius IQ. Rachel quickly learned that his sense of humor was not what she'd wanted. His nasty sarcasm disguised as humor fueled his narcissism. He twisted everything she said, which made her look stupid in front of others.

Rachel was a petite, darling woman with a toned body at the age of twenty-one when she married this man. He made sure they had no close relationship with family or her friends. He only allowed her to wear sexy clothing, including undergarments, and her primary responsibility was to be his arm candy. Before entering their frequent social events, he made sure to tell her just how fat and dumpy she looked. He'd ask her questions in front of everyone just to tell her she was wrong. In the car on the way home, he'd laugh and confirm she'd answered the question correctly the first time. His sick sense of humor was not what Rachel had in mind.

Rachel felt like a poodle on a leash. His sister even asked her why she stayed with him. After years of emotional abuse, Rachel thought she was crazy. Hugely successful at her job as the number one sales person in the country for a billion dollar company, she couldn't quite shake the thought that she was losing her mind. The stress of living with her husband took its toll. She'd find herself talking with others but could not hear what they were saying. One day she walked around a parking lot for two hours trying to locate her car. Later in therapy, she quickly learned she was not the crazy one. Her therapist told her she had two choices: stand up for herself or leave.

Rachel summoned her courage and told her husband the relationship was not working. He responded by saying that marriage was like a cross country drive – there are some potholes along the way. Rachel replied, "The f…ing bridge is out." They argued. He finally agreed to one therapy session. When the therapist told him she understood that Rachel had been emotionally abused throughout the two year marriage and asked him if it was true, he said yes. Although clearly confirming his own damaging behavior, he would not return to work on his issues, in spite of the therapist's warning that without substantial changes, his behavior would continue to destroy any relationship he had.

Shortly thereafter, Rachel secretly rented her own apartment and moved out. She went grocery shopping alone for the first time and felt paralyzed as she gripped the shopping cart. The knowledge that she could buy anything she wanted to eat was overwhelming. Her husband had dictated what and how to do everything. He told her not only what to wear, but also what to eat. She hadn't been able to have a Christmas tree because he didn't want one, and it wouldn't fit on the roof of his Corvette. That winter, Rachel bought a six foot Christmas tree. She dragged it for two blocks and put it up in her tiny apartment.

The night she moved into her own place, she went to her college reunion. "Oh my God," was her first thought upon meeting Joe. They both felt the immediate connection, but Rachel wanted nothing to do with men. Not yet. She later learned he'd moved to Chicago and decided to call him. He let her know he had tried to contact her as well. They talked on the phone as friends for several months. When he sent her Leo Buscaglia books, they were both dating other people and calling each other to discuss and laugh about their "bad" dates.

As their friendship continued, they finally began dating each other. When Joe asked her to move in with him, Rachel said, "I like my own place. I'm with you because I choose to be. If you're gone tomorrow, I'll be sad; but I'll be fine because I love me more than I love you." Joe loved this. Rachel was the first non-clingy woman he'd dated.

Rachel said he was the first man who did not almost immediately "grab her boobs." He cooked dinner for her at his place, kissed her, held her hands, and promptly took her home at 2 a.m. She knew he truly liked her for who she was. This was a new experience for him as well since he'd never been friends with a woman. He admitted he married the first two women he'd dated.

When Joe asked Rachel to marry him, she said he first had to go to therapy to find out what his role had been in his two divorces, and he did. There were some bumps along the way, but they have been happily married for fourteen years. At their sunset wedding in Maui, barefoot and surrounded by family, Rachel sang *"Wind*

Beneath My Wings" to her new husband. Rachel says it's our own fault when we compromise ourselves or our standards. Our dreams are hidden in the vortex waiting for us to accept them as the gifts they are. Her parting advice: "Ask yourself how you want to feel."

They are best friends and still tell everyone they are newlyweds. Rachel also said they know how to fight fairly. They aren't afraid of someone leaving because of a difference of opinion. This works because of the solid foundation of character they each have. The trust is unquestionable. The respect for each other is enormous and un-battered by life's challenges. There's no attempt to change each other. They are together by choice, and this choice is one they make daily.

Owning your character is a personal choice you can make as you welcome the love of your life to join you. You're invited to consider carefully what character traits you will demonstrate and accept in a life partner.

Questions for Group Discussion

1. What values do you bring to the table in the context of a love relationship?
2. What values are non-negotiable for you?
3. How can you determine what your partner's values really are before making a commitment?
4. What actions or behaviors would you list as relationship deal breakers?

Questions for Self-Reflection

1. Did you compromise your own values in a past love relationship?
2. If so, how did that compromise contribute to the dissolution of the relationship?
3. What are your personal deal breakers?

Exercise: Make a list of values most important to you and discuss them openly with any future potential mates. Find out what they think about these values and ask them what's on their list. You may be surprised by the level of compatibility you share, or you may find little common ground. Either way you'll want to know.

Chapter Three
Intimacy

Intimacy seems like a magical creature to me – like a tiny beautiful winged fairy so delicate and ethereal. I used to believe it would fly away at any moment. If I tried to catch it or hold on too tightly, it might be seriously injured or even die. In the past, I craved intimacy, yet harbored a silent fear about its very existence. My view of intimacy made me think it couldn't be real or sustainable in a love relationship.

Though I didn't have much hope for experiencing intimacy, I still wanted it. I wanted to feel true intimacy spiritually, physically, emotionally, and intellectually with my life partner. I think it's what most women want from a long-term relationship. Perhaps that's true for men as well. When intimacy is missing, the quality of the relationship suffers on many levels. An optimist by nature, I wanted to have it all, including a completely satisfying, intimate relationship with someone who felt the same way – someone who absolutely loved and adored me. For a long time, I thought that was too much to ask, especially since it probably didn't exist anyway, except in the movies.

Here's what Dictionary.com says about intimacy: "a close, familiar and usually affectionate or loving personal relationship with another person or group; a detailed knowledge or deep understanding of a place, subject, period of time, etc." Having a detailed knowledge and deep understanding of another takes time and a desire to invest oneself in the development of the relationship.

Accepting and/or giving intimacy on one or two levels is what we do with friends, business associates, doctors, and any number of other people we encounter. There is financial intimacy with our tax attorney and accountants. A type of physical intimacy exists with our doctor. We share spiritual intimacy with like-minded friends or church attendees. Intellectual intimacy is part of our connection with work colleagues, and we express emotional intimacy at various levels, depending on the people and the circumstances.

Some level of intimacy is expected in those situations, but it's easy to become confused about the level of intimacy we are enjoying when it comes to a love relationship. It is also easy to assume the existence of intimacy on all levels when in reality there is no basis for that assumption. For example, sharing physical intimacy does not guarantee any other intimacies are present or will develop.

The women I interviewed ranked sexual connection very high on the list of characteristics in the top five areas of attraction for their partners. While this is understandable and essential for relationship longevity, physical intimacy is especially powerful. In *Why Him, Why Her?,* Dr. Helen Fisher says that several chemicals, the feel-good hormones, are released during orgasm. This can engender a false belief that there is more intimacy than really exists.

Having an intellectually stimulating conversation over dinner may have established rapport leading to a feeling of intellectual intimacy, but that doesn't mean other levels of intimacy will automatically follow. It's sad to watch this assumption in play in the myriad of dating or relationship programs on television.

Women are often left asking questions about why he isn't pursuing them for a continuation of the relationship when they had such an enjoyable evening together. They invariably ask, often through tears, what they did wrong. Unless their table manners were atrocious, they behaved badly or had too much alcohol, the answer most often is "nothing." They did nothing wrong. Their dinner partner simply had no interest in pursuing a relationship. It is good to know this sooner rather than later in a relationship – before one person's investment outweighs any possible benefits.

We all crave intimacies at various levels in our relationships. Connections with our friends, family, social circles, religious affiliations, doctors, hairdressers, etc., all serve to fill our lives with that feeling of being part of something larger than ourselves. Many studies have demonstrated that people live much longer and are healthier when they regularly have intimate connections with a circle of others. No doubt, a variety of intimate relationships are necessary and fulfilling, but most of us want what I call the ultimate intimate relationship with the one other person with whom we can share our lives in all ways.

women I interviewed, and I came to have a love relationship most of us thought was impossible. You may be doubtful as hat's understandable. By sharing my experience, perspective and the stories of other women, I hope you will consider revisiting the possibility. I can unequivocally say that having spiritual, physical, emotional and intellectual intimacy with my husband has been a revelation and the most wonderful, satisfying journey – one for which I have immeasurable gratitude. I can breathe and relax and be who I really am, always in complete trust that I am unconditionally loved. I hope you are inspired by the stories of women who wanted and now have this deep level of intimacy, too. I invite you to consider how you might conspire with the *Universal Creative Energy Source, Spirt, God – whatever term suits you* to co-create true love in your own life.

I believe the purpose of our lives on this planet, in this space and time, is to come fully into the realization of who we are as individuals. When you become a happy, whole person who loves and respects yourself, you are in the best possible position to share your life with someone else on any level you choose. No one is needed to complete you. No one is needed to make you whole or to make you anything. You, yourself, are enough. When you feel whole and genuinely happy, you can share that with someone else freely and joyfully. The truth is that you certainly can't give away what you don't have.

I invite you to consider this next story, looking closely at what Kelly thought was possible in her love relationships. Like many women, Kelly was disappointed in how her marriage turned out. Therefore, after the divorce she decided to settle for less than true intimacy. Kelly is a fun loving, highly successful entrepreneur with a generous spirit. She knows how to take a lemon and make lemonade. However, I'm sure she'd tell you her life was still missing a special ingredient until she opened her heart to the possibility of true intimacy with a wonderful man.

"I had closed myself to the possibility of finding one single man for a committed relationship. When I fully opened my eyes, he was there right in front of me."

Kelly

Kelly's Story

"I just wanted to date a contractor," Kelly said laughing. Her house, which she lovingly referred to as the *money pit,* had innumerable things that needed to be repaired. Kelly had divorced her husband, Brian of twenty-one years and remained single for nine years following. During that time she'd fallen into what she calls, "event dating." She had a list of men she could call to accompany her on a variety of social occasions… one for rock concerts, one for black tie events, one for sporting events, etc. This worked quite well most of the time. It was tons of fun with no commitments.

Kelly, her husband Brian, and their friends John and Sarah had known each other since they were seventeen. Kelly and Brian were the first ones John and Sarah told they were getting married. They remained friends for many years until Kelly and Brian divorced and the relationships shifted. Brian was the bartender at their favorite hang-out. As often happens, people take sides and friendships change. During this time, Sarah became seriously ill. When her condition progressively worsened, Sarah unfortunately passed away. Their friend, John, had lost his mother, brother, and wife by the time he was forty-seven years old. He was alone and needed support more than ever.

After a few months, John started coming over to assist in home repairs at the money pit. Kelly had known him all these years, but she never had any thoughts about him other than friendship. Several months later, when John asked Kelly on a date, her reaction was not favorable. She told me her internal response was "Oh, no." Being friends was the only paradigm she'd had for this relationship. Quite frankly, his hanging around was beginning to be bothersome. Kelly continued to feel this way, but John did not stop with his visits, helping with house repairs, and eventually becoming one of her "event escorts."

One day, out of the blue, Kelly's favorite ex-boyfriend called and asked her to join him for a long weekend with friends in the mountains. Kelly was happy to hear from him and quickly accepted. They'd always had so much fun together. Before she left on her trip, though, John said he wanted to talk. Very calmly and respectfully he said, "I am not interested in competing for you. If this event dating is what you really want for your life, I'll understand, but I won't continue being part of it." Kelly was quite surprised since no man had ever told her so clearly what he wanted. Nevertheless, she departed for a weekend of fun and frolic in the mountains.

She wasn't planning to return until late Sunday afternoon, but early that morning she abruptly awoke and decided to leave. She couldn't wait to get back into cell phone range so she could call John. They talked for hours as she drove home. That day she decided to give a love relationship with John a chance. By listening to her heart, she realized how much she wanted to leave her friends just to hear his voice. They had so much in common, especially their quirky sense of humor, often laughing uproariously at each other's silly jokes.

After two weeks together, John left for an out of town business trip. When he returned, he arrived at her door with a single red rose. *He was a keeper.* Kelly had closed herself off from the possibility of finding one single man for a committed relationship; but when she fully opened her eyes, she was able to see him right in front of her. She told me this is the most comfortable relationship she's ever had. Every Friday he sends her a virtual rose; and each time they travel, he has real roses waiting for her in the hotel room.

If they had both been single years ago, Kelly says they would not have been a good couple. "I had to learn what I needed to learn. Most of all, I had to learn how to be happy myself," she said. John told her that he knew he was in love with her the night he saw her speak at a charity benefit she'd organized to celebrate her first ten years in business. He realized how she'd grown into such an amazing mature woman who was deeply generous - giving back to others in need from her business success.

Finding your own happiness and adding gratitude for what you both bring to the table is a powerful combination. It's not the roses - real or virtual, single or by the dozen - that count. It's who brings them.

A rose was an especially big deal for John. When he was young and married to Sarah, he excitedly brought home a bouquet of roses to celebrate their one month anniversary. They were financially struggling at the time and certainly had no money for this type of extravagance, but John so wanted to give his bride a romantic token of his love. She was furious and caused such a negative scene that he never gave her roses again. There were no anniversary celebrations. That's how she wanted it. They reportedly had a happy marriage, but how sad for John to have his lovely gesture so angrily rebuffed.

That's why it means so much to him and to Kelly, even when the rose is virtual. They've been together for years now, and this recognition of their love never fails to make her heart smile. He says, "You make my heart soar – that's s-o-a-r, not s-o-r-e." (One of the silly jokes at which they both laugh)

This story illustrates what can happen when women settle for one or two levels of intimacy. The outcome can change so dramatically when they open to the possibility of wholeness in their relationships. When Kelly stopped long enough to consider what John had to offer, she wisely decided to follow her heart and received true intimacy. The sparkle in her eyes and the smile on her face as she tells me her story is all the evidence I need to know she's connected with the love of her life.

Questions for Group Discussion

1. Is one of the four types of intimacy more important to you than any other type? For example: do you value physical intimacy over intellectual intimacy?
2. What type of intimacy was Kelly trying to avoid in her "event dating?"
3. What activities might foster increased intimacy in a love relationship?

Hint: Happy couples share feelings, goals, experiences, time, challenges, plans, success and failures.

4. What area of intimacy is most likely to wane first?
5. What are some red flags that might indicate an area of intimacy is slipping away?

Questions for Self-Reflection

1. Take a few minutes to think about the various types of intimacy (physical, emotional, intellectual and spiritual) in the context of a past love relationship. How do you feel about the intimate connection with your partner in each type?
2. How did lack of intimacy on any of these levels affect your relationship?
3. Did lack of intimacy in one area affect intimacy in other areas of your relationship?
4. Which type intimacy are you most uncomfortable discussing with your date/mate?
5. What types of intimacy to you want to improve for yourself before entering into another love relationship?
6. What do you want to do differently in your next relationship to create and sustain true intimacy?

Chapter Four

Authenticity

I once read an article about Melanie Griffith and Don Johnson, Hollywood actors who had been married, divorced, and remarried. After they divorced for a second time, Melanie said one of their favorite things to do had been to go out for steak tartare. Then she said something astonishing. "I don't even like steak tartare." Wow! What a revelation! She didn't even like this dish, and yet she'd been pretending to love it – all in a misguided attempt to please her husband.

The danger in this type pretense is that you may end up with the things you don't like playing prevalent roles in your daily life. It won't get any better once you're married or in a long-term relationship. In fact, you'll probably find yourself wishing you'd been more honest about your likes and dislikes. No one needs to pretend to like everything a perspective partner likes. You might want to think about this the next time you are tempted to say you also prefer something just because he does.

Pretending to be someone you're not will eventually sap your energy and leave you in an inauthentic relationship. For example, you may know women who aren't well endowed, but they wear highly padded push up bras hoping to look like they are. Predictably, they attract men who have a strong preference for large busted women. What do you think happens when that bra finally comes off? I wouldn't count on the longevity of that relationship. It may not fail because of the smaller than expected breasts, but the deception will most certainly become an issue. Trying to be someone you are not may attract someone's attention, but it's most likely a recipe for unhappiness and relationship difficulties.

One of the keys to satisfaction and longevity in relationships is walking in the truth of who you truly are. The other person must love you for who you are if the relationship has any chance of being successful.

Rachel, whom you met earlier, said she felt like she was living a life of deception until she decided to stand up and speak for herself. She was a capable businesswoman who allowed her first husband to dictate the smallest and largest details of her life. Rachel wanted to sing, maybe even perform professionally on stage or in a rock band. Giving up those passions and prematurely leaving her music education to please her husband caused Rachel to feel like she was living someone else's life. For years, she coped with her misery by smoking pot. She had several affairs, one of which resulted in an abortion; and generally she lived a life incongruent with her core values and true passions.

When Rachel met the love of her life, there was no question in her mind that she would tell him everything. She wanted an authentic life and an authentic relationship based on trust and love in the light of full disclosure. When she shared her life story over dinner one night, she expected him to get up and leave. He stayed because he knew the value of authenticity and the harm that comes from pretending to be someone other than who you are. Disclosing the past that you've now moved beyond is foundational for building a lasting relationship.

Living in fear that your partner may someday find out you did things he or she may not approve of sets a tension in motion that can destroy the very core of the relationship you're trying to build. Fear of being judged is hurtful. When your spouse or significant other knows your mistakes, your triumphs, and your life's journey more fully, both of you are free to relax and enjoy the next phase of life together. However, that doesn't mean you need to know every intimate detail about your significant other's life experiences.

If your boyfriend wants to know how many men you've slept with, tell him it's none of his business. The fact that you've had previous love relationships is enough. Men who persist in thinking women are sluts if they've had multiple sexual partners are living a life of double standard. That doesn't mean you have to do the same. Authentic men understand this and spend their energy dealing with more important issues.

What you reveal to another is a very personal decision that only you can determine. Don't hide things if you're concerned about how you'll feel if they are later discovered. Experiencing a negative reaction from someone you love and feeling judged are painful experiences, but it's better to find out early in the relationship. Besides, the energy it takes to pretend you were an angel when you might have been a wild child isn't worth it. Remember, if a man loves you, nothing will get in his way of being with you. That includes your past.

We expect authenticity in everyday life. If we order a bison burger, we don't accept a turkey burger instead. Finding out a diamond ring is really cubic zirconium is unacceptable. We all expect things to be as advertised. Disappointment comes quickly when deceit enters the picture. The same holds true for communication within any relationship.

When dating a new person, you should be sure to make authentic conversation one of your standards. If a man lies about himself from the beginning, it's a red flag - sending a warning that something isn't quite right. While I'm not an advocate of divulging your entire life story early in a relationship, it's important to get to know each other first. As a result, a rhythm develops that evolves naturally over time, and you'll know what to reveal at the appropriate time. As a relationship progresses, so does information sharing.

Talking and doing things together is the way people find out if they are compatible and if they want to continue being in each other's company. Any pretense gets in the way of that natural progression.

When her first husband said he shared her strong family values, Faun, who you'll meet later, thought that included spending time with them. Turns out, he was telling her what she wanted to hear and believe. In reality, he wanted to control her life by distancing her from the very support and love she valued so much. She married him after a short romance when she was still quite young and recovering from a family drama. Had she stopped to find her center and evaluate the authenticity of his words, she might have discovered how empty those statements were and discovered his true agenda.

Taking time to know what is real and what is fiction is important for developing a connection sustained by mutual trust in honesty and love. Listening to your inner voice is the final barometer on any situation. Advice from others is great and often helps us define what we want to do, but that should not supersede our inner knowing or intuition.

No one, but the couple themselves, knows what's inside a personal relationship. They may appear to be the perfect couple with the ideal relationship. Yet, without mutual respect, trust and authenticity, most relationships will likely falter and perhaps collapse under the strain. When a relationship is missing the solid foundation of authenticity, it can't stand the test of time. In the end, it will bring far less than envisioned.

The next story illustrates what can happen, even if it takes many years, when feelings are pushed aside for what everyone else thinks. Wendy didn't start her marriage with any pretenses, except for one small detail. She wasn't completely sure she was in love with her soon-to-be husband.

According to her family, he was a good catch, and they'd readily accepted him. She didn't think she had any real reason to end her plans, so ignoring her hesitation; she went ahead with the wedding. Like most people who choose marriage, Wendy's intentions were good. She was determined to try hard to make it work. Over the years she'd watched her sisters experience painful divorces. No way was she joining them. Her story is an example of what can happen when authenticity finally wins.

After you read her story, you may want to take time to think about what might be happening in your life that may not be the highest and best demonstration of authenticity.

"I spent so many years walking around on eggshells, afraid of saying or doing the wrong thing. Now I can just be myself."

Wendy

Wendy's Story

Wendy says it doesn't work to marry someone thinking you can fall in love with him. She married a man she respected and her family accepted, but somewhere in the recesses of her heart she knew it wasn't complete love. She thought she would grow to love him as they spent time building their family and lives together. Thirty-three years later, she threw in the towel and left.

Why did she stay so long? Of course, she stayed for the children. They're always part of any divorce decision, but they were grown and out of the house by then. Since several of her sisters had been through divorces, Wendy was determined to be the one who made it work. This is a testament to a woman's strength and perseverance and probably total acceptance of the old adage that marriage is hard work.

After the divorce, Wendy felt great relief and started planning her new life as a single woman. She was at peace with herself and her decision even though her children were incredulous that this could have happened. Although she wasn't looking for a new relationship, one day she hoped to find someone she could be totally in love with. It happened when she least expected it.

One night her sister asked her to join a group of friends for drinks and dinner at a local restaurant. Wendy was a bit early. She sat at the bar sipping a glass of wine, when a very good looking man came in and sat farther down the bar. Because her sister hadn't arrived yet, Wendy didn't know if the good looking man was part of the dinner group.

After a short while, the man (Grayson) came over to say hello, surmising she might be there for the same event. When he touched her arm, well that was it. Wendy said she knew there was a connection the moment he touched her. Much to her delight, they sat beside each other at dinner and immediately found much in common. There was only one small problem – her sister had actually invited him to meet one of her single friends who'd planned to join them later.

When the other woman arrived, Grayson, ever the gentleman, spent time talking with her as well. But he knew whom he was really interested in pursuing. Grayson and Wendy quickly started dating and have been happily married for twelve years. It took time for Wendy's children to accept their parent's divorce. It also took them a while to accept the new man in their mother's life. One day, several years into her new marriage, Wendy's son said since Grayson had come into her life she looked happier than he'd ever seen her. That was her sign that her children had embraced her new life.

"I can just be myself with Grayson," Wendy said at the end of our interview. She spent so many years not being able to say or do the things she wanted – always wondering what was next, not having that deep feeling of ultimate trust in her relationship. The underlying tension caused problems on many levels. Thirty-three years is a very long time to feel less than happy and satisfied. It can feel like an eternity if you're not being your authentic self. It takes courage to walk out of a situation that isn't working, especially when no one in your family understands or supports you.

Wendy found the love of her life. She's free to be herself every day, knowing Grayson loves her for that very reason. He was also in a long-term marriage which had ended over a decade earlier. Although I did not interview him, I'm betting there are many similarities contributing to the break-up of his marriage.

Being yourself and having someone fall in love with you because of the things he finds sweet or adorable about you is exhilarating. Coupled with unconditional acceptance of your less-than endearing characteristics is what makes a relaxed, easy-flowing relationship. The joy and absence of constant tension is a strong foundation for relationships to flourish and deepen over time, even when life's little - and not so little - disasters happen.

Anyone who's been through a personal or family crisis knows how much it means to have a solid partner to count on – someone who's there for you on all levels: physically, emotionally, intellectually and spiritually. So instead of asking yourself, "What did I do wrong?" when your love relationship isn't working out, ask yourself if you are participating in the relationship from a place of authenticity.

Those who have a fully developed awareness of who they are, soon figure out when you're pretending to be someone you're not. Do you really want to give your time and energy to someone who turns out to be a different person from the one you've fallen for? I encourage you to take the time you need to know yourself. You need to become the type of person you want to be and to be clear about your own standards and values BEFORE you enter into an intimate love relationship. If you aren't clear on these things, you risk inviting the wrong people to share your life.

Questions for Group Discussion

1. What does it mean to be authentic in a love relationship?
2. What role does vulnerability play in becoming an authentic person?
3. Does being authentic in a relationship mean you have permission to behave badly?
4. Does being authentic mean you can disregard your mate's feelings, desires, or needs?

Questions for Self-Reflection

1. Have you ever felt like you had to be someone else in order to be loved?
2. What effect did this have on your relationship?
3. What effect did this have on you personally?
4. Are you afraid your potential mate won't be attracted to the authentic you?
5. What do you think might happen to your relationship if you demonstrate your true feelings?

Chapter Five

Trust

Having only five letters, the word "trust" seems like such a small word, maybe an overused word and already thoroughly understood and accepted as the basis for any type of thriving relationship. But trust is actually a huge word, one often given out freely in the absence of appropriate context. Trusting another person is a gift offered when it is earned through right action – not something carelessly assumed. Dictionary.com defines trust as: "assured reliance on the character, ability, strength, or truth of someone or something . . . confidence or as a condition of some relationship."

Being trustworthy is an essential element of character. It can't be skipped over or willed into place; it's derived from authenticity. When someone comes from a place of authenticity, there is a greater possibility we can rely on the trustworthiness of his/her character. The importance of trust was mentioned over and over in the interviews. Unfortunately, it was missing in many relationships, marriages and experiences.

The feeling of trust or confidence - so often talked about - was not present without context or basis. In fact, it was just the opposite. The women who knew they had trust with their partners knew it because they'd seen, heard, and felt the genuine and essential nature of their partner.

If a man is interested in you, he will pursue you – he will call you if he says he will. If he's said he'll call you and he doesn't, he wasn't being truthful. He didn't lose your number. He's not interested and he wasn't man enough to let you know. He didn't fail to follow-up with you because of anything minor you did wrong. He's just not into you. Why waste your time? There are other choices – better choices.

Trust is like credit. It should only be given to those with whom we've established a basis for return. The consequences of extending credit to those unable to pay can result in a downward economic spiral. Giving credit to those with no evidence or resources to meet their obligations is like throwing money away. Handing out your trust without any evidence of reciprocity is similar to giving credit without a credit check. It may feel equitable and generous; however, the result can be devastating, similar to what happened with the American banking system. Trust is the credit you are offering another when you have the knowledge that he/she possesses the resources to reciprocate.

In a new relationship, trust begins at point zero. Starting at zero means you have no information or basis for offering your trust. Like a temperature gauge, there are negative markers as well as positive ones. As you move through the relationship, each instance that surfaces on the trust side moves a person's credit to the positive side of the scale. Each instance that surfaces on the distrust side moves their credit rating to a negative reading. That is the purpose of dating – a critical tool in building a trusting bond with another.

Getting to know our prospective partners allows us to assess the measure of trust we can extend to them. If you don't take time to talk with and see another person in action, you've limited your ability to effectively see and experience his/her trustworthiness. Some people are not worthy of your trust, even in the most basic ways.

If a man lies to you from the first moments or days of a possible relationship, he is not trustworthy. When a man knows right away you have standards and he's interested in you, he will most likely live up to those standards from a foundation of his own integrity. He will do what he says and over time provide you with a basis for giving him your gift of trust.

There are tons of players in the dating world. Many men, motivated mainly by their desires for sex, don't have an interest in knowing who you are. It's doubtful they're interested in having a relationship with anyone. Are you extending your trust to them prematurely? Offering one of your most precious gifts to a stranger and expecting something in return almost always leads to disappointment, heartbreak, or worse.

Being able to trust someone in an intimate relationship is truly a wonderful gift, but there is a vital precursor - trusting yourself. What happened along the way that makes some women trust others long before they trust themselves? Nancy trusted her friends and family when they told her what a great match she was making in her first marriage. She wasn't sure, but instead of trusting herself, she went ahead with the marriage and spent thirty plus years walking around on pins and needles, not knowing what he was going to do or say next to create drama. Nancy was afraid to be herself for fear of launching a tidal wave of unpleasantness.

For a variety of reasons including ignorance and religious beliefs, most of us did not learn the critical skill of trusting ourselves. We were not given this vital piece of information - no one should be able to impose his/her will on another, especially in a love relationship. As Nancy painfully learned, not knowing what you are coming home to on a daily basis quickly erodes trust.

We learned many things in school and from our parents and mentors. One thing I don't remember being taught was the importance of trusting myself. I talked with quite a few women about this, and they too wished they'd known much earlier how to trust themselves. That's not to belie the importance of seeking input or advice. But since you're the one who has to live with the outcome, you're the one who needs to make the final decision – in love and life.

One wise woman said she is teaching her daughter to ask herself how things make her feel. If you are entering a new relationship, you might want to ask yourself a few feeling-centered questions. For example, how do you feel when you are with this person? How do you feel when you see him in action? How do you feel when he looks at you? You know the answers to these questions before you can articulate them into words. Develop your instincts and learn to trust them.

Tune in to how you are feeling. The next time you are about to do something that sends an unsettled queasy feeling to your stomach, take the time to evaluate the situation. This begins the process of learning how to trust yourself, and over time it becomes a natural and more effective tool allowing you to make the best decisions for your highest and best life.

Learning to trust your own instincts means trusting your intuition. Contrary to past popular belief, intuition is not something only women possess. In the time when thinking was valued over feeling, this gift was known as women's intuition, an interesting way to devalue its significance and deem intuition as inferior to reasoning. No wonder women rejected or undervalued its role.

Owning our intuition as the birthplace of trusting ourselves has been revived. Rolling eyes and condescending smiles no longer stifle this conversation. It's more than okay to trust your intuition, it's positively necessary. The more you trust your intuition, the stronger it becomes. As you learn to trust your intuition, you'll also notice your confidence growing, which will support your decision-making process. Truly confident women know they deserve better than an untrustworthy man. They know that trust is an assured reliance on the truth.

Learning to trust yourself is a gift only you can give. It comes before trusting others. When you see it in yourself, you'll recognize it in others. You can walk away when words and actions are in conflict. You can set the standard high for having a trustworthy relationship. Men who don't have this characteristic won't stand a chance with you because they'll soon learn there are no compromises on this critical value; trust is non-negotiable.

Almost every woman I interviewed talked about trust having birthed and sustained their relationship. Not having it ultimately unraveled the relationship, sometimes one strand at a time.

Bridget's story is about growing up in an environment so bereft of trust she almost didn't survive childhood. Lack of trust followed her every relationship until she awakened and decided not only to trust herself, but also to allow herself to trust another. Bridget is a real spitfire of a woman with a disarming English accent and tons of energy. She shares a snippet of her journey, hoping to inspire others who've been wounded to overcome the past and welcome in true love.

"Trust comes from the heart and I trust him with my heart. I cherish him and he cherishes me."

Bridget

Bridget's Story

No one had ever been there for Bridget. Her biological father deserted the family; her mother couldn't cope and sent her to live with her grandparents. Life didn't improve much after that. Her childhood was hellish by anyone's standards. Therefore, predictably she fell in love and married while she was very young. She'd moved from England to the United States, hoping for a new beginning. Soon after, she met and married a nice man who was protective and made her feel safe.

Although there was no foreign language to learn, Bridget had a very hard time adjusting to the new environment. An extrovert by nature, she still found making friends as difficult as remembering which side of the road to drive on. Her marriage was the first real stability she'd ever known, but what she thought was a safe haven changed as soon as she started to mature.

As long as supper was on the table on time and she was at home when he arrived, things were relatively okay. As Bridget developed a circle of friends and became more comfortable in her own skin, the relationship with her husband became more challenging. She couldn't even attend a weekend church retreat without incident. When a friend drove her home afterwards instead of allowing her husband to pick her up in the church parking lot, there was an argument.

He routinely complained and criticized Bridget and her friends, increasing his efforts to completely control her every move. Once he even picked the grocery receipt out of the trash to be sure she hadn't written the check for ten dollars over for cash. Several times he threatened to cancel her car insurance so she couldn't drive. He even threatened divorce when he was upset, fully knowing the horrific abandonment issues she faced during childhood.

Bridget was focused on fitting in most of the time, so she never developed trust for herself or anyone else. Her main goal was not to "piss off anyone" for fear of rejection. She lived each day in survival mode.

After years of enduring this emotional rollercoaster Bridget had enough. One day while her husband was being unfairly critical, she looked at him and said, "Shut up Rick, just shut up." He looked at her as if she was a mute who had just spoken for the first time. As she claimed her voice and herself, she tried to communicate to her husband what wasn't working in their marriage. He continued his relentless criticism and threatened to leave her once again. Fed up, Bridget replied, "The next time you say that you'd better be ready to leave."

On that note, he moved out of their bedroom she thought in spite, only to return several days later. Bridget promptly moved into the basement. She felt as though her spirit was dying. She longed for the nourishment that comes from true intimacy with another. "In fact, he didn't even like me," Bridget relayed. After their divorce, he told her family that she must be a lesbian or on drugs.

This rocky road of marriage ended after ten years and two children. Bridget, like so many of us, tried hard to make it work. When she realized it was not going to get any better, that her very soul was shriveling, she knew her decision was correct.

"I was going to turn into a *"Stepford Wife"* if I stayed," she said. He was re-married within six months and introduced his new wife to his children as "their new mother." If that wasn't bad enough, her ex-husband and his new wife began a campaign to treat Bridget as if she was a "complete screw-up." Now she says, "I could have become the first woman President of the United States, and still there would have been no acknowledgement of me as a person or as the mother of our two children."

Bridget had quite a few issues to work through and she did – healing one step at a time. She did the work, gained her peace of mind, and was enjoying a measure of happiness for the first time in her life. She'd even let go of worrying about finding a mate. Instead, a colleague introduced her to a singles group focused on recovery from bad relationships. This worked so well for her she began working as a volunteer to help others through the process. The group planned bi-annual social activities. The next event was a Halloween costume party, which Bridget loved.

Always a fun loving woman, Bridget dressed as a "biker chick" for the party. She wore a long red wig, skull cap, and short skirt with fishnet stockings – anything that emphasized the stereotypical accessories one might think of for this costume.

The man she was unknowingly about to meet, Vincent, dressed as a member of the Blues Brothers, came with a friend, not having been part of the singles group. He began talking to Bridget and her girlfriend. They talked for quite a while. Soon, Bridget noticed another woman staring at them from a distance. She thought perhaps she was with Vincent. Her glaring became mildly disconcerting as Bridget did not want to be seen as trying to hit on someone else's date.

When Vincent asked her to dance, she couldn't say no. They danced and continued talking. He asked if he could call her when he returned from his skiing trip that weekend. She said yes, but no one had a pen. They both mingled with the group but somehow always ended up together talking, the other woman still staring or glaring at them as Bridget recalled.

The situation became awkward and Bridget and her friend decided it was time to leave. Vincent said he had a pen in his truck so he walked out with them. On the way they ran right into the "other woman" and a group of her friends. To be polite, they all stopped to talk. After a few minutes, Bridget decided she just had to go ahead and leave. It wouldn't be appropriate for this woman to see Vincent taking her phone number. As it turned out, the other woman was an acquaintance with an eye for Vincent, but the feeling was not mutual.

That was Friday night. On Sunday evening, Vincent called her. How he obtained her number she didn't know. They agreed to go out to the movies, a movie so bad they ended the evening talking and laughing about it. Vincent had been concerned it might have offended Bridget and he apologized for taking her without really knowing what it was about. Bridget understood and found the whole situation to be hilarious. They began dating and were married a year and a half later. It's been fourteen years, and he's very much the love of her life and she is his.

The love connection became clear to Bridget shortly after meeting Vincent. One of the reasons she gives is their mutual decision to get to know each other as friends first without sex involved to distract them. After getting to know Bridget, I think this created a much needed safe space for her to be able to relax and be herself. That was critically important for her given the childhood traumas she'd been through.

Not feeling safe had been a way of life, a place dreaded, yet she was unaccustomed to anything else. Knowing what you need is only the first step in getting there. Vincent must have truly sensed this and provided the safe haven for their relationship to grow. He was there for her, a new experience for Bridget. No one had been completely there for her when she needed them, so she had no expectation it could actually happen.

That changed when her father in England, who had come in and out of her life, became seriously ill. Bridget went back and forth for several visits and again when he passed away. At that same time, she was also travelling frequently for flight attendant training. Through everything, Vincent was there for her, a supportive rock she never had before. From the very beginning of their relationship he demonstrated trustworthiness – something she wasn't even sure could exist.

You may have noticed from the story that a trustworthy man did not enter Bridget's life until she started to have trust in her own decisions. Developing this quality within, opened her eyes to recognize it in another. If this sounds strange, think about the last new car you purchased and how many cars just like yours you then began to notice. Becoming aware of trust in action opens the channel for receiving more of the same – an example of the *Law of Attraction.*

Questions for Group Discussion

1. The author says that giving your trust fully to someone you don't know is like giving them your credit card. Do you agree?
2. Can a breach of trust with a love relationship partner ever be repaired?
3. Is trust something we instinctively feel with another person or is it best developed over time?
4. What could a couple do to develop trust early in a relationship?

Questions for Self-Reflection

1. Have you ever trusted a love relationship partner and been betrayed?
2. Do you trust yourself to make good decisions with respect to love partnership choices?
3. What will you need in order to fully open your heart to love again?
4. Are you willing to set healthy boundaries in your next love relationship?

Chapter Six
Gratitude

An attitude of gratitude is essential if you want to attract and sustain a quality love relationship. Gratitude is like a magnet attracting that for which you give thanks. You don't need to take my word for it; you can prove it for yourself. Whether you are consistently practicing gratitude in your life or are new to the concept, I encourage you to read this chapter with an open mind and consider adopting an attitude of gratitude with renewed commitment.

My life changed considerably for the better when I decided to try it. When I learned about the power of practicing gratitude, I wasn't too happy with my life circumstances. In fact, I was quite practiced in the art of feeling sorry for myself, and I complained constantly to my friends and family about how difficult and unpleasant my life had become. Embracing gratitude created space for another world view and allowed the anger and resentment I felt to fade away, almost before I realized what was happening.

When I thought about writing this chapter, I knew I wanted to share with you what the word gratitude means to me. As I reflected on this simple, yet transformational concept, I decided to use the letters in the word itself to describe its personal meaning in my life. I hope you enjoy my definition and take time to reflect on what gratitude has meant or can mean for you. And remember - gratitude is a foundational building block for attracting and sustaining an authentic love relationship.

G for Generosity: Having an attitude of gratitude engenders a spirit of generosity. When we take time to feel deep appreciation for all that we are and have, we can quickly relax into a natural feeling of generosity towards ourselves and others. It's easier to feel connected when we understand our own humanity. We all have gifts we didn't earn and we've all fallen short in expressing our appreciation for both the gift and the givers. This is easily corrected.

For example, tuning into the beauty of nature always catapults me into the feeling of generosity both for others and for me.

A day rarely goes by without an expression of gratitude for the gift of an extraordinary man with whom I share my life. As a couple, we're generous with our mutual appreciation for everything we do to support one another. It's not uncommon for us to talk daily about our gratitude for being brought together, as well as for the life we've built and enjoy. We're committed to living in a state of gratitude. This attitude keeps us connected emotionally, intellectually, spiritually, and physically.

R for Reciprocity: My husband and I love this word, reciprocity – a mutual giving and receiving. Each of us had previous relationships in which reciprocity was severely lacking. Our similar experiences birthed a new reality for our relationship. We treasure this concept and take action daily to sustain reciprocity in our lives together. For example, working from home affords me the luxury of cooking breakfast for my husband during the work week. He lovingly reciprocates by cooking our weekend breakfasts. When he prepares dinner, I am his sous chef and vice versa. These small examples set the tone for how we live our lives together with reciprocity.

We know how it hurts to be taken for granted and feel unappreciated. Not wanting to repeat experiences from our past relationships, we decided to practice reciprocity in our gratitude for one another's contributions to our marriage from the very beginning. When a couple shares "substantial compatibility," a term you'll learn more about in the next chapter, the desire for reciprocity naturally evolves. Any feelings of unbalance in our relationship are discussed before they cause unnecessary conflict.

Reciprocity requires both a balanced giver and a receiver in order to work. So often women are more comfortable being givers and do not know how to properly respond when they find themselves in the unfamiliar role of receiver. Start now to graciously accept any assistance, gift and expression of gratitude that comes your way. A simple thank you is all that is necessary. Practice relaxing into the flow of giving and receiving.

A for Attitude: We all have a personal approach to life that begins when we start each new day. It's easy to become stuck in a habit of dreading what lies ahead. Instead we can greet each day as a gift and remember to feel great gratitude for another opportunity to live and contribute.

Therefore, rather than leap out of bed at the sound of your alarm clock, why not pause for five minutes and feel gratitude for everything. We all have so much for which we should be grateful: the warm bed that was available for sleep, your ability to work to support your family and other pursuits, your friends and family members, your home, the morning coffee or tea, or perhaps even the irritating boss who provides you with an opportunity to improve your patience and/or communication skills. What's on your list? The attitude you choose for every situation may well dictate its outcome.

T for Timeless: Here's the cool thing about gratitude – you can start any time you choose, even with the past. You may not have been grateful for many things experienced in your youth. You may not have expressed appreciation for all that your parents, family, or friends did for you. You may not yet appreciate the many things you have learned from past relationships.

It's not too late. You are still here on the planet if you are reading this book. It's possible to begin this instant by reflecting on all you appreciate in your life - both past and present. There truly is a silver cloud in every lining if you take time to look for it. I encourage you to give it a try. It's never too late to take a moment to express your gratitude to someone else. The more you practice doing this small act of kindness, the easier and more enjoyable it becomes.

I for Invitation: Adopting an attitude of gratitude opens an invitation to share your feelings with yourself and others. Many years ago when I first began practicing gratitude, I had an opportunity to see its effects on a cranky elderly woman. I was dazzled by what happened. It took less than five minutes to invite her into the higher energy vibration of gratitude.

It was the day before Thanksgiving. My then husband was in the hospital recovering from surgery. This unanticipated event had seriously interrupted my customary plans for shopping, preparing, and cooking. With two children and a sick husband to collect, I was rushing to pick-up the turkey in a packed grocery store when I overheard Miss Cranky complaining about everything – all the people, the long lines, the slow cashiers, and more. Her unhappy demeanor continued as she stood in line behind me. I decided to see if I could shift her attitude.

I turned around, caught her attention, and flashed my best smile. She forced a slight grin as I commented on how we were all in this last minute holiday shopping mayhem together. She readily agreed, and right away I let her know how happy I was to be able to purchase my turkey since my husband was in the hospital. She said, "Oh my." Then, before she could continue any complaints, I expressed my deep gratitude for being able to have my family at home for Thanksgiving under these circumstances.

Even though I had to do everything by myself, I was smiling and grateful. Her face relaxed and she began to shift her comments from complaining to sharing her empathy for me. She even agreed we were all blessed to be there, even with the long lines. I knew then my attitude of gratitude was something I could use to invite others into a happier place.

By viewing gratitude as an invitation for connection with the *Universal Creative Energy Source,* you can change your life and impact the lives of others. Won't you accept this invitation to shift your energetic vibration to a higher level? Again, you don't have to believe this will work; you only need to try it consistently over a period of time with sincerity. You can't fake emotion with the *Universal Creative Energy Source.* This is one of those moments that doesn't require extensive deliberation – just do it! Accept the invitation.

T for Transformational: Living in a state of gratitude will change your life. There are many research studies on the benefits of gratitude. As I read several of them, the similarities became obvious. People who consistently practice gratitude have better physical and psychological health, improved sleep, more empathy, increased happiness, and less stress and depression. This is just a partial list, but doesn't it sound like something we all desire? You can read these research studies or conduct your own personal research by diving into a daily gratitude practice. Are you ready for a changed life?

When I was originally introduced to this concept, I was in an unhappy place. Unsure if anything I did was going to work to improve my circumstances, I decided to try it. I discovered that spending time in gratitude meant less time worrying, fretting, and being fearful of what bad things might come to be. I learned it's not possible to be in fear while feeling grateful. I began to feel better much more rapidly than I'd ever thought possible. My energy shifted and my life circumstances followed. Of course this didn't happen right away, but in time I grew in my ability to stay grounded in the positive rather than dwell on the problems. Practicing an attitude of gratitude is truly transformational.

U for Understanding: Just as practicing gratitude fosters generosity and reciprocity, it also supports a deeper understanding of yourself and others. Stopping to say "thank you" - even to strangers - reminds us we are all humans muddling through life to the best of our abilities, given our level of knowledge at the time. Knowing this creates the space for increased understanding and less judgement.

Fully embracing a new concept or diving more deeply into something you already know may not be that difficult, but the challenge is in the consistent practice. The more profound experience of true understanding comes when we align mind, body, and spirit.

Practicing gratitude may sound simple. Yet, until we make it an integral part of our everyday experience by giving and receiving gratitude in the context of living, we won't harness its full potential. Like any other habit, it takes time to make or break. We can all decide today to trade in complaining and embrace thanking. That's how we can change the world and our love relationships.

D for Demonstration: In Faith Young's book, ***What Would Faith Do?***, she shares her coffee cup philosophy. Faith says when we reject someone's kind offer of a cup of coffee or tea, we are telling the *Universe* we don't need anything. Remember: if we want to attract more good into our lives, it's best to accept a gift - large or small - with great gratitude. This is a wise message indeed.

Women are especially prone to doing most of the giving in relationships through social conditioning. Isn't it time to learn to graciously accept a gift given from the heart so that we may participate in the abundance the *Universe* has to offer? Giving and receiving are but opposite sides of the same coin. This is often referred to as the *Law of Reciprocity.*

Faith also says that silent gratitude doesn't do anyone any good. We all like to hear a personal compliment or comment of appreciation. Why not start today by handing out a word of thanks with a smile. Researchers tell us that emotions are contagious. Think about that and try it out for yourself.

Our energetic vibration is affected by others with whom we come into contact. Think about a time when you walked into a room of angry or tense people. You most likely felt the heavy energy before you realized what was happening. Each of us can practice being a demonstration of happy, grateful energy. Also, for you singles, this high level of positive energy is where you'll find your ideal mate, unless you'd rather attract Mr. Grumpy.

E for Ease: The more we live in gratitude, the easier our lives become. Embracing this attitude allows us to relax and focus on all that's right with our lives. For singles ready to find their love connection, this may not be an easy path to begin. Practicing gratitude does take repetition over time and requires a positive attitude. I've seen women attempt to list what they want to be thankful for with resignation, rather than delight. This will not work. I want you to feel at ease when making your gratitude list. Include only what's real for you at the time. This practice will get easier with repetition and stopping to feel the results. Appreciate someone and watch their body language. You'll be hooked in no time.

Start your daily gratitude journal today. Don't think about it, just do it. The power in this process can be indescribable. You'll soon find yourself feeling grateful for everything in your life. As a result, – you'll be more relaxed, less stressed, have more confidence, enjoy more happiness, and have better love relationships. Singles, this is a skill you'll want to hone before attracting your love connection. Being grateful is one of the most important attributes to have in keeping a deeply satisfying marriage together.

If you're someone who has been scarred or traumatized by others' lack of love, you may find it difficult to open your heart. Being grateful for what you have starts a positive energy flow that can open your heart to giving and receiving love, regardless of your history.

I previously spent too much time feeling angry and frustrated about my life circumstances until I realized my feelings were attracting more of the same. By giving my energy to what I already had, all I loved and enjoyed, I was able to cultivate a space for personal growth, which attracted more positive relationships of every kind.

It's hard to feel gratitude when you're ruminating over everything that makes you angry. We often blame others for the struggles in our lives. However, at some point, it's time to let go of the past and start building a better, more positive life. That means you need to take full responsibility for your life. When it comes to love relationships, or any relationship, you're ultimately responsible for how you're being treated. Once you accept that concept, you empower yourself to change circumstances that don't serve you.

A wonderful outplacement counselor and mentor came into my life when I lost a job I really loved. I almost refused to see her the day I was shown the door. But thankfully, her supreme kindness and understanding allowed her to work with me from my place of self-pity and disbelief over a situation which I did not begin to understand.

Added to that was the disappointment and anger I felt about my personal life. My head was spinning. My insides were yelling, "What the hell happened here? No, I don't want to talk to an outplacement counselor! I'd really like to tell a few people what I really think of them." Fortunately, I had enough self-control to prevent an unnecessary encounter.

After weeks of stalling, I agreed to a meeting, which turned out to be the beginning of my new life. Her wisdom and compassion allowed me to stop, breathe, and take note of the truth before me. I had been lost in the darkness – too busy fuming over my circumstances to see that I could be thankful for so much, including the power to change those things that no longer worked for me.

Take the time to count your gifts and blessings. Make a list and add to it daily. You'll be happier as a result. You may have noticed that being in the company of uptight, frustrated, complainers is draining. That's why most people like to be with positive people. They're uplifting. Feeling gratitude changes your energy and can even shift the energy in your environment.

One of the central messages of this book concerns the creation of an environment in which we can thrive and evolve in our thinking, feeling, and doing. Practicing gratitude is a central tool in creating that environment. Having an attitude of gratitude is a habit that's well worth working on, especially if you know it's not one of your strengths. Being grateful for a partner's contribution to the relationship is a key ingredient not only to attracting, but also to keeping your special someone.

Think about how you feel when someone takes notice of something you've done. Giving that same appreciation back in a relationship builds strong bonds. If you want a happy, deeply satisfying and sustainable relationship, don't make the mistake of taking small gestures for granted. Say "thank you" for everything, especially the little things. If you want the flowers to continue after the dating moves to the next level, remember to practice gratitude and continue your romantic gestures.

You can start this habit now. Be grateful for your health, your home and family, your job, your car - anything you have that makes your life good. If you can truly count your blessings and feel gratitude, you open a positive energy flow from the *Universal Creative Energy Source* for your good.

Many women shared their viewpoints on this topic during their interviews, explaining how they appreciate all the things their husbands or partners do daily. They express their appreciation even though it's understood. One woman said, "I thank my husband for everything. I thank him for being such a good provider. I thank him for fixing the car when it is broken. I thank him for stopping what he is doing to catch a spider." This woman has been married to the love of her life for thirty-seven years, and she still has a sparkle in her eyes when she talks about him.

Remembering to be grateful puts a smile in your heart and on your face. If you want a partner that is happy and appreciative of your efforts, be a partner that is happy and appreciative. Positive energy attracts more positive energy. So resist the urge to focus on what you do not have today. Instead, find and focus on even the small things you do have. This helps to keep you in the positive energy zone where good things tend to happen. It can also bring more friends – more partner possibilities perhaps.

With no success, Kaitlin tried looking for a life partner in three different cities in three different states. When gratitude for what she did have took center stage, her life connected unexpectedly with another's. Observe her attitude of gratitude as you read her story and use it as a learning tool.

"I decided it was ok not to be married. I had everything I needed with none of the marital drama my friends were experiencing."

Kaitlin

Kaitlin's Story

Kaitlin loved being single. She'd decided very early, before entering college that she was going to focus on her career. Marriage and children were not in the immediate picture. Maybe someday, when she'd established herself as a successful professional, she would consider marriage. She didn't give the subject much thought; but when she did, she could not think of anything a man could give her that she didn't already have.

Her career took her all over the world. She comfortably supported herself financially, owned her home, and had great friends and family. She could go where she wanted, when she wanted, alone or with friends. Marriage was always something that would happen some other day. It never occurred to her that she'd spend her entire life without a partner, even though she never dated much. The one exception was her time as an exchange student in New Zealand. Since her Visa would expire, she knew a date wouldn't turn into a relationship. It was fun knowing no guy could derail her career plans.

Thirty became forty and Kaitlin knew she wasn't going to find a man without doing something to look for one. She moved three times in the next three years: first to Seattle, then to Los Angeles, and finally to Denver. She met another single woman in Seattle who was dating three times a week. Kaitlin finally decided to ask her how she did it. Great Expectations, she said, a popular dating service before the internet match websites became mainstream. Singles looked through volumes of pictures at their offices to choose a dating match. The deal was a three year membership for twenty-five hundred dollars. It took some convincing from her friend, but Kaitlin decided to give it a try. She certainly wasn't meeting any prospects by working all day in her home office.

Year one in Seattle produced no lasting results. The men she met often made her wish she'd just stayed home to watch her favorite television show. Year two in Los Angeles was not a good fit for Kaitlin in any sense of the word. Not only was she unhappy, but also the dates were a complete mismatch. In year three, she moved to Denver and almost instantly felt better. She was happy being home. The membership to Great Expectations expired and she chose not to renew. She'd had enough of that. Besides, after watching several friends go through divorces or suffer miserable marriages, she decided she was fine without all the drama.

Grateful for what she did have in her life, Kaitlin decided it was okay to be single. She relaxed into this decision as so many of the women I interviewed did, happily pursuing her own interests – no more worrying about marriage.

Since knitting was one of her hobbies, she decided to enroll in a weekend knitting retreat. You may be thinking – not a great idea for meeting men. However, before the weekend was over, one of the women at the retreat had invited Kaitlin to join her, her husband, and a group of friends for a night out to see the *Nutcracker Ballet*. Kaitlin agreed. After the performance, the group stopped at a local restaurant for dessert.

When no one introduced themselves, Kaitlin once again wished she'd gone home to watch television. The somber group sat around the large table, hardly saying a word. Kaitlin thought the outing had been a mistake. Then the door opened and in walked Jason and Jenny. Several people at the table looked up and said hello to Jason. Immediately the atmosphere came alive. Jason walked over to Kaitlin and said, "I don't believe we've met," introducing himself and his friend Jenny. They pulled chairs beside her and initiated a conversation which continued for hours, eventually relocating to the home of one of the group members.

How had this happened? The men all knew each other through their volleyball team. What about the other woman, Jenny? She was ten years younger than Jason, having recently returned from her Peace Corps assignment. They were just friends. During the conversation that evening, Kaitlin mentioned one of the downsides to working alone in her home office. There was no one to go out with for Friday night Happy Hour. Jason gave her his business card and said he'd like to join her for Happy Hour the following Friday.

Kaitlin thought she was making a nice new friend. She'd enjoyed talking with Jason and looked forward to their meeting. However, they both travelled frequently and had a few scheduling challenges for meeting again. They decided on lunch, which was quickly followed by an evening date and talking until 2 a.m. Soon after, they began to spend time together almost daily.

Two months later Jason left for a week's vacation with his buddies, a plan he'd made prior to meeting Kaitlin. In the past, Kaitlin's strong need for alone time had often left her feeling suffocated by the men she dated. This time was different. She missed his company. He was the first man that did not make her crave more time alone.

They've been married for sixteen years, working together as well. Jason told Jenny the first night he met Kaitlin that this was the woman he was going to marry. It wasn't that immediate for Kaitlin. She'd become accustomed to not being part of a couple. Since she wasn't looking or expecting it, she attracted this love relationship from her acceptance and gratitude for a fulfilling life, rather than engaging in a desperate search for a partner.

Questions for Group Discussion

1. What does having an attitude of gratitude mean to you?
2. What are the possible benefits of living in a conscious state of gratitude?
3. Do you have any personal life changing experiences of living in a state of gratitude?
4. Do you currently have a daily gratitude practice or journal?

Questions for Self-Reflection

1. When is the last time you expressed gratitude or appreciation for someone in your life or for an act of kindness shown to you?
2. Can you think of a time when feeling deep gratitude or appreciation positively impacted a personal situation?
3. Do you take time to appreciate the little things your partner does to support your relationship?

Exercise: Each night before you go to bed, make a list of 3-5 things for which you feel gratitude or appreciation. Add to the list each night, making an effort to choose different objects, people, and experiences. Don't forget to include yourself!

Helpful hint: Try sharing your gratitude list with your partner as a daily ritual.

Chapter Seven

Compatibility

Compatibility is another important aspect of building a solid relationship. Lack of it can lead to "irreconcilable differences," the language used in divorce filings. Having a strong measure of compatibility is a basic need for long-term partnership happiness. In modern relationships, compatibility has a front row seat.

My grandmother once told me in her youth a woman was quite pleased to find a man who kept himself clean, didn't drink too much, and brought home the paycheck. Obviously, the evolution of relationships has drastically changed what today's women are looking for in a potential mate. We want a partner to share our lives with on many levels. When I talked to happily coupled women, the majority stated how important it was to share time engaged in activities together. Those activities included everything from talking, to leisure activities, and to sex. Even doing nothing required a solid measure of compatibility.

There are many ways to become seriously connected or disconnected in a love relationship. In my first marriage, I erroneously added our common backgrounds to my important values list and thought I had a recipe for compatibility. We were raised in the same religion, shared common family values; he was educated and worked for a solid company in a management position. His well-appointed apartment was immaculate and he could prepare an excellent meal. My family was somewhat concerned about our ten year age difference, yet pleased with the match. What a terrific basis for a long-term partnership.

What I failed to know, understand, or recognize was our incompatibility on several levels. For example, we did not agree on financial goals, spiritual direction for our family, or on how to spend our leisure time - to name just a few. There were red flags early in the relationship which I ignored. Emotional intimacy between us was on shaky ground. A red flag of incompatibility was waved in my face when during our long-term relationship he purchased a house without any input or involvement from me. My feelings were hurt, but I stuffed them inside and overlooked the obvious message. Although my list contained valuable compatible traits, they were not enough to sustain our marriage over the long haul.

The word compatibility means capable of existing together in harmony, meaning to agree consistently. Harmony is a great way to describe the essence of compatibility. In the music world, harmony is the simultaneous combination of tones. It doesn't mean that everyone is singing or playing the same note, but the music or song works together brilliantly. A high degree of compatibility between two people creates harmony, even during the challenges. The less compatible a couple is, the more opportunities there are for discord.

Another metaphor for understanding compatibility is the old fashioned weighted measuring scale. If there is a significant imbalance on one end, the scale is tipped in favor of one side. Many women spoke to me about the imbalance they felt in their first relationships and how very different it is now that they are more equally joined with their life partners. When couples are "substantially compatible," differences are not disregarded or dissolved as much as they are respected and honored for the role they play. Many differences don't cause struggle because they're not important. For example, a couple can have different hobbies, tastes in food, cars, friends, etc. However, there are differences that carry more weight. Money, sex and children are frequently topics of serious disagreement between couples.

Family finances, once the exclusive purview of men, are now more openly and regularly discussed among high functioning couples. For most of us, full financial disclosure and agreement is non-negotiable. When a couple has an equitable partnership, there is no need for secrets about finances.

Being open about the family income and budget is the beginning, but the issue doesn't stop there. When there is no agreement on how the resources are being allocated and expended, controversy ensues. Secrecy and resentment compound the problem, creating an environment ripe for possible financial disaster. Frank discussion about financial priorities, including spending styles and savings goals, before making that ultimate commitment, is a good-sense practice. Continuing to meet and discuss finances throughout the relationship creates trust and supports emotional intimacy.

Absence of sexual compatibility can be another relationship disappointment. The topic was certainly taboo for hundreds of years. Even today, when we are more open about our lives, it is still not easy to discuss. Most of the women in my survey highly valued sexual connection with their partner, regardless of the length of their relationship. Lack of sexual intimacy was a sure sign of discontent. While not a focus of the research or interviews, this was often listed as an important factor in overall relationship satisfaction.

Relationships often fail because of major differences in the quality and quantity of physical intimacy. Talking about it early and anytime one partner isn't happy with how it's going is not easy, but it is definitely necessary. There are many informative books and research on this topic if assistance is needed to start the conversation. Although discussing sexuality sooner is better than later, it's never too late to talk about your sex life. When sex is great, it's a small percentage of relationship satisfaction; but when it's bad, the issue can overwhelm an otherwise satisfying partnership.

For anyone who has children, you know all too well how much drama can ensue over differing parenting styles. Even discussing whether there will be children can be a challenge. Assumptions are not a good plan when it comes to this subject. If you want children and he doesn't, you're not likely to talk him into changing his mind after you're married. Even if you successfully change his mind, resentment may creep into the relationship in later years.

Don't waste your time. Put your energy into connecting with someone who wants to be a parent. Parenting is a lifelong deal and comes with challenges. Sometimes you want to send the little darlings back to where they came from. (Note to my children: Don't get offended, it was only a fleeting thought – a few times. I wouldn't trade you for anything, really).

Children from first marriages affect a second marriage. That's a reality couples need to consider. Being on the same page is enormously important to avoid unnecessary conflict. This isn't easy, even if you've agreed on how and who will handle the many challenges. Issues will arise that weren't discussed earlier simply because you didn't envision them ever happening in your relationship.

When you and your partner have significant compatibility on your side, working through the challenges is much easier. A friend once confided to me that her second marriage unraveled because of the amount of money he spent on his children. The differing parenting styles and lifestyle choices was too much for the relationship to bear. Hindsight is illuminating, but foresight lights the way for avoiding these types of pitfalls.

My husband and I feel we have a measure of compatibility that serves us well in daily living and in planning for our future. We both experienced the opposite situation in our previous relationships and believe our compatible lifestyles, financial priorities, moral values, leisure activities, and intellectual pursuits make our life together rich, whole, and always exciting. We can talk about anything. We can disagree without acrimony. We willingly support each other in all of our endeavors, both individually and as a team. The importance of this cannot be overestimated, even though we have several differences. The balance is tipped to the side of compatibility on most things, so our differences complement, rather than weaken, our bond. As a result, we spend most of our time enjoying life, not figuring out how to compromise or give in to the other's opposing wishes.

Theresa's story beautifully illustrates how the outcome changes when two people really communicate and get to know each other more deeply, falling in love from a place of awareness and genuine compatibility. As you read her story, you'll see how the absence of compatibility initially created disconnection in their relationship. While many couples don't know how or don't want to take the time to discern possible differences, you'll find this story demonstrates just how vital it is to have this knowledge before making a long-term commitment.

"I knew he was the one because of how I felt when I was with him. . .we had so much in common."

Theresa

Theresa's Story

Theresa married her first husband when she was twenty-three. They'd planned to be married sometime in the future; but when an opportunity came along for them to live and work in Saudi Arabia, she enthusiastically said yes. The fantastic position he'd been offered required them to be married in order for her to accompany him. As a result, they accelerated the wedding date. It was the chance of a lifetime to realize their dream of living abroad.

All was well at first, but over the next five years he became increasingly controlling to the point of not letting her out of the house without him. What was once an exciting new adventure had become more like a prison. Because divorce was not part of her family culture, Theresa resigned herself to the situation, hoping things would improve. She vowed to try harder to accept what she thought must be the normal challenges of being married. After all, she'd been told that marriage is not a "bed of roses." Theresa thought this must be the thorny part.

His incessant controlling behavior continued despite her best efforts. She finally decided she'd had enough and began to plan her escape. The obstacles she had to overcome included the distance from family and living in a foreign country. To make things more difficult, the company they both worked for held their passports. In order for Theresa to get hers, she needed her husband's approval. He rarely travelled to the U.S., but thankfully a few months later he was offered just such a trip.

They decided he'd travel ahead and Theresa would join him several weeks later. That was her chance. She'd already contacted an attorney in the States and had a plan. Now she had to get her passport. In order for her plan to work, she needed to leave Saudi Arabia three days earlier than previously agreed upon. She explained the change in dates to her husband's secretary and miraculously was given her passport to freedom.

After the divorce, Theresa decided she would focus on her career. She set a goal to become vice president of a major corporation. Although she dated off and on, she wasn't open to a long-term relationship. She didn't trust herself or any of the men she met. In her heart, she wanted a husband and a family. Instead, she focused her energy on her career. Then unexpectedly everything changed.

Theresa enjoyed an enlightened and fun group of female friends who were practicing "visioning" in their lives. Many companies develop vision statements to help their employees better understand future goals and objectives for the company. Having a personal vision about where you want to be is a similar powerful tool for obtaining personal goals. Visioning can also come in the form of meditating and allowing the *Universe* to bring your heart's desire. During a meditation one day, Theresa had a strong vision of a man and a child. At the time, she wasn't sure what it meant.

Theresa lived in Washington, D.C. and sometimes travelled to California for business. On one of her trips, she discovered that one of her colleagues had lost his wife to a serious illness. She barely knew him, but she'd always thought the tall, handsome, tanned man was "a bit full of himself." Nevertheless, she felt great compassion for him and decided to express her condolences.

The only two rules Theresa had about dating were: no dating anyone she worked with and no long distance relationships. As the old saying goes, "Never say never."

Later that evening Theresa decided to go for a walk with David, the man who'd lost his wife. They walked on the beach outside the hotel where they had been sequestered all day in meetings, followed by a social function. After talking to him for a while, she realized that he was a very nice man, not at all what her first impressions had been. When the meetings were over, they both went their separate ways. On the flight back to D.C., she realized she'd let her guard down during their beach conversations.

Shortly after she returned, she received a letter from David. She didn't answer it for a month. Personal issues around being hurt and fear of intimacy came up for her, so she took some time to deal with them before responding. When she finally answered his letter, she said she wanted to be friends first and get to know him. He called as soon as he got her letter. He was happy to hear from her as he had begun to think she hadn't been too impressed by him. Their communication via letters continued.

A few months later he came to Washington to spend time with Teresa. There they made plans for her to go to California two months later to meet his two year old son, Jay. David and his first wife had wanted children, but she had been too ill to carry a child, so they'd adopted. During this visit, Theresa had an experience she will always remember. While playing with his son, she picked him up, and he laid his head on her shoulder. At that moment, Theresa knew this was her child. She thought to herself, "I don't know what I'm going to do if this man does not ask me to marry him. I know this child is mine and we are a family."

Later that week, Theresa and David went for a walk in the park while the baby was visiting his grandparents. David looked at her and said, "What would you say if I asked you to marry me?" Theresa said, "I don't know, you have to ask me first." David smiled and asked her to be his wife.

They were married five and a half months after their first conversation. Jay called her mommy from the moment the wedding was complete. That was over twenty years ago, and they are still having a wonderful time together. Theresa moved from Washington, D. C. to California because of the family support there for Jay, but before the move she was offered the corporate Vice-President's position she'd always wanted. She happily turned it down for her new life and family in California.

Theresa told me her heart had longed for a family, but she'd closed herself off to that possibility after feeling the hurt and disappointment from her first marriage and the commitment to focus solely on her career. She also said that although she'd dated a few men, she knew they just weren't right. Fortunately, she hadn't settled.

Questions for Group Discussion

1. The author says "substantial compatibility" is important for a long-term sustainable love relationship. Do you agree?
2. What does the concept of "substantial compatibility" mean to you?
3. Can couples be "substantially incompatible" and still have a happy marriage?

Questions for Self-Reflection

1. How would you rate your level of "substantial compatibility" with your last love relationship partner?
2. Do you think areas of incompatibility were the cause of your break-up?

Exercise: Make a list of things, activities, values and experiences that you and your partner shared as areas of compatibility and a list of areas of incompatibility. Which list is longer?

Hint: Having a longer list of areas of compatibility is the meaning of "substantial compatibility."

Chapter Eight

Part I Conclusion

In the first two chapters of this section the link between character and intimacy was established with character as the foundation for building a life of true intimacy with another. The next three chapters: *Authenticity, Trust* and *Gratitude,* discuss a few of the vital elements of character and are not designed to be conclusive. We all should decide for ourselves what qualities, traits or components of character we value in ourselves and others. These are examples for your consideration. The chapter on *Compatibility* concluded this section to underscore the beauty of sharing life with someone who walks by your side through mountaintop experiences and through the valleys as well.

The following story depicts Helen's long journey to freedom and happiness. Like most of the women in this book, including me, she had to learn many life lessons the hard way. It may be true that each of us has to learn some things by being hit in the head with a two-by-four, metaphorically speaking. However, challenges in life don't always have to be unnecessarily difficult. Hopefully, the stories on these pages have created a guide for you to walk a smoother life path.

These stories are presented not merely as a means to convey what went terribly wrong, but rather to illuminate the way forward to a delightful experience of true love and total intimacy with another grounded in character. I hope the common threads in each of these stories have emerged in a way that inspires and influences us to strive for the qualities we wish to see and can count on in ourselves and in our partners. Spend time determining for yourself what qualities mean the most to you, and then allow them to create your standards.

In this final story of Part I, Helen, a lovely, talented writer and editor, has been on this planet for seventy-three years, although she claims she's thirty-seven and younger than several of her children.

I tell you this because Helen not only had significant challenges in her personal life, but also she was a professional businesswoman in a time when most women in the workplace were merely secretaries.

Workplace struggles included being told her small pay raise was "What most women get," and was given without a performance review. When Helen stood up for herself, and for all the women who followed her, insisting on a fair review of her work, the boss's boss gave her a pay raise equivalent to the top male performer, over fourteen percent. This was one of many issues Helen faced while working, often as a single mother raising four children. As you will see, instead of love and support, she also had serious challenges at home.

"Once you discover your strength, you're never the same person."

Helen

Helen's Story

Helen met her first husband, just prior to graduating from high school, shortly after ending a three-year romantic relationship. Since Rich's family was in need of financial support, he'd dropped out of high school to go to work after his freshman year. He was driving a yellow Corvette the day he met Helen and her girlfriend and offered them a ride back to school after lunch. They accepted the ride, but he said "no" when they suggested skipping the rest of the day in favor of a longer drive.

Subsequently, Rich asked Helen out for a date. When she declined, he asked her girlfriend. When that didn't work out, he persisted and Helen finally agreed to a date. Shortly after becoming a couple, Rich's extreme jealousy surfaced. Helen was young and thought he'd change with time and he did. His jealousy worsened.

They were married for twenty-two years and had four children. They lived in a large home and enjoyed a supportive church community, including numerous social activities. From the outside, their life appeared to be normal, but Helen described her personal and emotional life as "hell." She never knew who was going to be in the room with her. One minute Rich was fine, the next he was alarmingly different. Eventually he was diagnosed with a mental illness, but he refused to talk to the doctor or take any medication.

Helen's job required interviewing people for local news stories. They had great friends, often visiting each other's homes; but no man could step foot inside the door when Helen was home alone. Any contact she had with another man sparked a jealous rage from her husband. This situation created a myriad of professional hardships for Helen.

One day, she came home to find an envelope on the mantel containing evidence he had cancelled all of her medical insurance and removed her name as beneficiary on his life insurance policies. He'd also started drinking after work, coming home later and later, usually drunk.

The final straw came the night he staggered in and said, "If I find the SOB that's wrecking my marriage, I'm going to kill him." Helen brilliantly replied, "Go look in the mirror." One week later, she asked him to leave, fearing for her children and their safety.

Once Helen found her strength, she knew things would never be the same.

Over the years, Helen had various jobs at the newspaper, sometimes working at home to be with her children. She'd been hired by Tim, the Bureau Chief of the regional newspaper for six counties. He was a very nice man with a disruptive home life Helen described as worse than hers. His mentally ill wife was also prone to fits of jealous rage. On one occasion she'd even cut his business suits into pieces. Part of his job was also interviewing people. Since his wife did not trust him to talk with other women, she often threw temper tantrums. Tim stayed with his jealous wife until his daughter graduated from high school. After that, he'd had all he could take and ended his marriage.

Helen had known Tim for almost five years and enjoyed his friendship. She knew his personal situation and respected his decision to stay married until his daughter graduated. When Tim was free, both he and Helen slowly opened their hearts to more than friendship.

They were married in her living room twenty-eight years ago. They happily give each other total freedom to be themselves. Their past experiences brought the realization that the jealousy and lack of trust they'd had to endure was not about them. Neither had given their spouse cause to be jealous. Both Tim and Helen had been fully committed to their marriages and tried very hard to make them work.

Helen was bitterly disappointed and angry when she realized there was no other choice. She had never wanted a divorce. However, she knew without a doubt, her marriage was not going to improve. Always hopeful, she endured the abuse for many years before finally deciding to leave.

She described what she has with Tim as the complete opposite of her first marriage. This experience painfully illustrates that marriage doesn't thrive in the absence of trust. Her advice: "Give each other freedom to be yourselves."

Helen's story is about a woman of character, devoted to her husband and children, a community volunteer, a warm and caring friend and neighbor whose intention was to live a full and happy life. Her "essential nature," though incompletely described here, is illumined through her journey. Her efforts to be a loving, supportive wife were met with serious character flaws from her husband when he took his money, time and affections to the bar, indulging in the excessive consumption of liquor.

Helen and her children were robbed of true intimacy. He wasn't physically present to be a father or husband much of the time. When he was there, his outrages created fear for their physical safety. When normal adult conversations suddenly turned irrational within the span of minutes, intellectual and emotional intimacy rapidly dissolved. What may have begun as spiritual intimacy with their church and community activities became merely a façade for others to see because Rich's behavior at home was nothing like his reputation.

He'd become an entirely different person from the man she'd married. Helen was unable to conduct life as her authentic self, unable to even talk with another man. Her fear of retribution stifled both her personal and professional life. The trust they once shared quickly evaporated when he began spending their discretionary income on alcohol and illegally attempted to remove her health benefits. I'm sure these are only two of the many examples that contributed to the erosion of trust in her life partner.

For many years, Helen felt only bitterness for the dissolution of her dreams. She felt gratitude was a nice concept, mainly for other people whose lives hadn't turned out so miserably. You can see from her story that compatibility on any level: physical, financial, emotional, spiritual or intellectual had gone long before the marriage legally ended. When a woman can't talk to her partner in love without fear, what's left?

As Helen released the bitterness and claimed her own life, walking in the truth of her being, the love connection she desired manifested. Awakening in her own time in her own way she reached out to touch and hold the hand of her beloved. Tim and Helen enjoy an equal partnership with all four types of intimacy supported by authenticity and trust.

Part II

It's All About You

Chapter Nine

Forget About It

Almost every day I meet or hear about single people searching for their special someone. Internet dating sites have proliferated as popular vehicles for the search. Reality shows bring the quest into our living rooms with shows like *The Bachelor* and *The Bachelorette* surviving season after season. The show may conclude with declarations of true love and proposals of marriage, but the results most often crumble when the cameras are gone and the reality of everyday life in more ordinary circumstances returns. Many others spend their leisure time in clubs dancing and drinking, desperately seeking a real connection.

Steve Harvey used the phrase "sport fishing," in his book, *Act Like a Lady, Think Like a Man*. According to Harvey, when a man is sport fishing, he plans to throw you back into the sea in spite of his admiration for you. If you want to be a "keeper" it's critical to take back your power and stand in a place of clarity that honors your standards and values. If your strategy isn't working, think about changing it. After all, you always have a choice when it comes to your life.

If you wouldn't go to a hardware store to get a haircut, you might want to think about why you're looking for the person of your dreams on the piers of sports fishermen. The odds are against success. If you're out on the town for a fun night at a club, that's one thing. You may even meet a wonderful person. But consider the bar scene is probably not fertile ground for finding a life partner.

The first step in finding your special someone is to forget about it. Yes, forget about finding your life partner – for now. Intense drive, desperation, and obsessing do not create the positive energy necessary to attract a stable, fulfilling relationship. In fact, engaging in such a search creates dis-ease and angst that inevitably brings more failed attempts and disappointments. When that happens, a successful match can seem further and further from reality. If you find any of this fits you, stop. Take a recess from the search for now.

You may be thinking, "Why would I do that when I'm not getting any younger and I'm lonely?" Spending nights, holidays, and weekends alone can be depressing. However, the more you focus on what you do not have, the greater the chance of creating more of the same. Remember the gratitude model; practice being grateful for what you do have. Heartfelt gratitude opens the door for the *Universe* to co-create with you your heart's desires through the *Law of Attraction*.

The following quote from Abraham Hicks is one of my favorite explanations of the *Law of Attraction*. You may want to copy this quote and post it in a prominent place so you can read it every day or mark this page in your book. "If you let your dominant intention be to revise and improve the content of the story you tell every day of your life, it is our absolute promise to you that your life will become that ever-improving story. For by the powerful *Law of Attraction* – the essence of that which is like unto itself is drawn – it must be."

In this chapter and throughout the next three chapters I'm going to give you a powerful step-by-step plan to assist you in writing a new story. Your story will become that which you desire most deeply. The tools and exercises described in this book are designed to help you move away from focusing on what has not happened for you in a love relationship. Let's find out what is holding you back. I hope you will embrace this process giving it your time, attention, and intention to shift your thoughts, beliefs, and actions. Let's get started!

The process begins by forgetting about it. Taking a recess changes your energy and aides you in releasing the struggle. Letting go of what has not worked is essential for opening the pathway to welcome in true love. It's not about searching and struggling. After interviewing scores of women and thoroughly examining my own experience, I discovered "forgetting about it" a common thread for those who connected with the love of their life.

As you prepare the way to receive that which you have desired, your energy will attract the love of your life. By taking this time for yourself, you'll gain peace and clarity. Through the steps in this section, you'll hone your standards and values and polish the relationship qualities you have to offer. Taking this time for yourself is not a detour – it is the road ahead, the one leading to the destination of your heart's desire. If you've been all over the map going in every direction, take this rest stop.

The latest research on quantum physics confirms the world is made up of energy. The smallest particle forming all matter is pure energy, including each of us. Tension, worry, and stress create negative energy. If you are struggling and fretting, you are emanating and surrounding yourself with negative energy. Negative energy attracts more of the same. It's important for you to position yourself to attract what you want for your life. This is true in all aspects of your life. In order for the *Law of Attraction* to work the way you want it to, negative thoughts of lack need to be replaced by other more positive intentions.

If you feel like every encounter is going to be less than you hoped for, you're right. If you feel like your next boyfriend will just be another loser with irksome flaws, you're right. If you have high hopes about the next prospect you meet, but feel the underlying stress that it will probably not work out, right again. Even if you believe it will be great, you may be so tense about it and expect so much that your energy slips into the negative and creates more reasons to be tense. This is not an effective way to attract your beloved, as you've no-doubt already experienced.

While on your hiatus from looking for Mr. Right, take the time and space to feel the peace, relaxation, and joy you want in your life. Victoria did just that. After spending too much time worrying about her crumbling marriage and the prospects of being alone raising a child by herself, she finally let the relationship go.

Following her divorce, she made a life changing decision to forget about relationships. Instead, she set out to create a happy new life for herself and her daughter. She made a plan, bought a new house, and focused on her business. She gave no thought whatsoever to finding a new partner. As you read Victoria's story, notice how her conscious decision to forget about it actually freed her from the angst she'd felt for years, allowing the *Universe* to bring the true love of her heart's desire.

"I didn't know where I was emotionally with men. I needed time – a break for my mind to re-evaluate."

Victoria

Victoria's Story

Everything had finally fallen into place. Victoria had just gotten out of her distressing marriage and purchased her first house alone. Her business was going well and added to the relief she felt, being on her own with her daughter. She felt quite proud of her independence. Keeping the focus on her business and raising her daughter occupied most of her time. No way was finding a new man necessary, she thought.

She'd married an older man when she was quite young, and although he taught her many valuable lessons about the realities of life, the marriage wasn't sustainable. What Victoria had initially interpreted as his desire to care for and protect her had become controlling instead. His infidelities added to their mounting problems and took its toll on their relationship.

Just as Victoria realized the truth about her marriage, she learned they were expecting a child. That news was the tipping point in her decision to stay. She was determined to continue trying to make it work, but nothing changed in spite of her efforts. The split had been inevitable; Victoria didn't need or want a domineering partner in her life.

Victoria and Sandy had been friends for years and their daughters often played together. Sandy and her recently divorced brother Clark were planning a party with friends and family when Sandy decided to invite Victoria. Victoria says she doesn't remember at all why, but Sandy arranged a time for a phone conversation between her and Clark to discuss something important about the upcoming weekend. Victoria had never met Clark, but apparently there was a good reason she needed to talk with him. She found out much later that her daughter and her little friend were also involved in the plot for the two of them to meet.

The phone rang as previously arranged, and suddenly Victoria received a message - the voice in her head was clear. She said, "I know this makes no sense whatsoever, but this thought came to me out of the blue. If I pick up the phone and talk to this man, he will be the one I marry." That was quite the jarring thought since she had no intentions of starting a new relationship. Marriage was the farthest thing from her mind. Somehow she managed to pick up the phone when Clark was calling. They had a short conversation and that was it. However, she knew it would not be their last.

They lived hundreds of miles apart in two different states; but when the *Universe* conspires, nothing can stop it from delivering your love to you. Clark was laid off from his work three weeks after meeting Victoria. Three months later, he moved four hundred miles to be with her. They were married two years later and have been happily together for twelve years. According to Victoria, their love continues to get better every day.

It may not make sense to anyone else, but Victoria knew he was the one after talking to him that first time on the phone. The comfort level was "built in," she said. There was no turning back for either of them.

Like most of the women I interviewed, Victoria was not looking for a new romance when it walked right into her life. She wanted an intimate relationship someday, but it was not on her priority list at the time. The divorce had been difficult, and she didn't think it was fair to her daughter to bring a new man into their lives.

After meeting Clark, Victoria had to re-think her stance. Once she really knew Clark and witnessed the type of person he was, she decided it would be crazy to let such a good thing go. The host of red flags that should have been blinding in her first marriage was nowhere to be found this time.

Part of finding your special someone is being open to the possibility and being ready should it occur, even though it's not on your "to do" list. Making unnecessary rules and being closed to the possibilities is like putting roadblocks on a journey you've yet to begin. Listen to your intuition. You'll be surprised at what can happen in your life if you stay open to the opportunities and refuse to fret over your current circumstances.

At the beginning of this chapter I said that most relationships crumble when the reality of everyday life returns for *The Bachelor* and *The Bachelorette* contestants. While this is true in most every case, one woman did find the love of her life on a reality television show. As you read Trista Sutter's story, think about what she may have done differently from many of the other contestants whose relationships ended in disappointment.

"Don't sell yourself short – don't settle.
There is someone out there for everyone"

Trista Sutter

Trista's Story

They became friends in the eighth grade, bonding quickly through mutual interests and the similar experiences of parents divorcing. He lived with his mother and she with hers. Throughout high school they were the fantasy couple. He was the football team quarterback and she was a pompom girl. Both were funny and attractive. He was usually the life of the party and they had a great time together; but after four years, they separated when he decided it was time to spread his wings and date other women.

The young man across the street from Trista's Sorority House captured her heart. Although she'd been raised in a religious family, her devotion had faded over the years. He brought spirituality back into her life as they regularly attended Bible study and church services together. Like her previous boyfriend, he was athletic, social, and intelligent. Trista loved his family as much as her family loved him.

He was a great guy and she valued her family's opinion of him, but she also wanted to begin a graduate degree program in physical therapy with a highly ranked college in the field. This would mean a long distance romance, at least for a while. Moving to Miami spelled the end of their three year relationship as Trista met new people and realized she wanted more.

In graduate school yet another handsome, social, athletic man entered her life. He was two years younger, and a year behind her in the same program, but they had many similar interests. It was not uncommon for them to share a computer – his big mistake and her good fortune. An email from one of his friends clearly indicated he'd been seeing another woman. When confronted, he calmly said he had no idea what she was talking about. His innocent face must have been convincing – Trista decided to stay. Shortly after this incident she discovered a female friend who'd come to visit had been more than just a friend. This time she permanently ended the relationship.

There were a few casual dates as graduate school was almost over, but Trista had no real interest in pursuing a relationship with any of them. What Trista did next would change the course of her life. She answered an ad for a new reality television show. She was chosen as one of twenty-five women to appear on the *Bachelor*. Each week, women were sent home by "the bachelor" until there were only two remaining, one of whom was Trista. She had fallen for the handsome bachelor, Alex, and she was convinced that he'd fallen for her as well. Two days prior to the final rose ceremony, he told her she would be the chosen one.

You may have watched as the unthinkable happened. Unexpectedly sent home without the rose or the ring, she was devastated, "bawling her eyes out" for two days. At this point in the show the focus is on the final couple. There was to be no more contact between the jilted runner-up and the bachelor. But Trista was heartbroken and wanted a final conversation. Why had this happened? She really wanted answers.

During the taping of the show she'd become friends with the producers. Seeing her pain they finally relented to her pleas for a conversation with Alex, but only if it would be taped. A phone call was arranged and Alex, feeling badly about the situation and his possible error in judgment, pushed for continuing the talk in her hotel room. Trista knew she could not agree to this without the producer's permission. The answer was a definite "no." Their denial of his request was a gift Trista had yet to recognize.

Three months later and just as the first episode of *The Bachelor* was airing, Trista received a call from the producers asking if she would consider accepting the role of *The Bachelorette* on their next show. Of course she would do it. It would be so much fun to live in a mansion, meet twenty-five new guys, and enjoy fantasy dates. Her boss didn't quite agree and said "no" when Trista asked for another leave of absence. Feeling like she'd been stuck in a rut, she quit her job and headed to the new show. Alex had seemed like the perfect guy on paper, but now she was thanking *God* the producers hadn't let them meet again that night. He definitely was not the right one for her.

Before the nationwide search began for twenty-five eligible bachelors for the new show, Trista was given a battery of personality tests and met for long conversations with a psychologist to determine the type of man she would find attractive. By the end of this process she thought they might know more about the type of man she wanted than she did. If you've watched the show, you know that bachelors leave each week until only a few remain.

The final four bachelors had hometown dates with Trista where she met their families and friends. She was falling for Ryan, the handsome firefighter from Vail, Colorado. He took her to the fire station to meet his co-workers and then onto a gondola ride high in the mountains. There, he kissed her for the first time on the wedding deck.

Ryan cleverly slipped a note into her pocket while they were in the limousine with no cameras rolling. It was down to the final three contestants, but Trista was thinking only of Ryan, even when she was with the others. She took him and one other man, Charlie, to meet her parents.

When she later learned that Ryan had taken her father aside and asked his permission to propose, Trista knew a dream was coming true. At heart, she was very much a traditional woman who, since childhood, held the picture of her future husband asking her father for his blessing. Trista was in love with Ryan, not Charlie, and not anyone else she'd dated on this show. When she was with him she felt safe and comfortable. The final rose was his and the beautiful ring was hers. They were engaged that night and married a year later. Trista's face beamed with deep happiness as she shared her story with me which now includes two adorable children.

The marriage of Ryan and Trista Sutter stands in stark contrast to the outcomes of most of *The Bachelor* and *The Bachelorette* shows that followed. She admits to being caught up in the situation, wanting to be the chosen one during *The Bachelor* show. She is so thankful it didn't happen for her then. She learned valuable lessons from the experience and went into the next show knowing there was a possibility of finding true love, but also knowing if it did not happen she would be fine. She was hopeful, not desperate.

Her advice:

"Don't sell yourself short – don't settle. There is someone out there for everyone. They may not be the CEO of a company or someone everyone else thinks is perfect.

"They may not have what society deems perfect - movie star good looks, an overflowing bank account, or an elite circle of friends; but more importantly, they'll make you laugh, feel safe and share your values.

"Go with your gut, not what everyone else tells you!"

It definitely was not an accident that Trista met the love of her life when she was thirty years old, after forgetting about the search, embracing her own happiness, and trusting her instincts.

LOVE COACHING PROGRAM

It's ALL About YOU

PERSONAL PLANNER

STEP ONE: **Forget About It** (Recess from Dating)

Begin your personal Love Coaching Program by committing to a period of recess from dating. This time-out is essential for you to be able to change the dating patterns that have not resulted in your love connection. Commit to taking this hiatus for yourself while you complete the Love Coaching Program outlined in this book. This will help you get off the unproductive dating circuit and give you the critical time you need to shift your beliefs and outcomes. It's important for you to follow the activities below while taking this recess.

Exercise 1: Begin a daily gratitude practice: For the next two weeks take each letter of your name and write a minimum of one gratitude statement each day. You can also write a complete set each day using all of the letters of your name. ***Note:*** The purpose of structuring the gratitude exercise in this way is to help you get started. If you already have a gratitude practice in place, this method will help you to think about it in a different way, hopefully adding to your creativity.

Example:

G Guacamole I had yesterday

A Alterations on my new dress

Y Yes to date night

L Loving hug from grandchild

A Allowing myself to rest

W Writing a new blog post

I Implementing more exercise

C Crazy Colorado weather

K Keeping my sense of humor

Exercise 2: Read this list each night before you go to bed. Note: Thinking of all the things you're grateful for will put you in a state of relaxation that will help you sleep.

Exercise 3: Write your own, *Why I am Still Single Story.* Include what you tell yourself, your friends, and your family about why you are still single (preferably one page or less). Since this exercise asks you to reflect on the reality of your story, please take time to do this in a place of quiet and comfort. The deeper you go, the more you'll get out of doing this particular exercise. Your personal, *Why I am Still Single Story,* is a key foundation for the remainder of this program. I've included an example below:

Why I Am Still Single

My mother asked me again for the four hundredth time what's going on with me, why am I not dating. Maybe she secretly thinks I'm gay, I don't know. Maybe it would be easier if I were. I told her I just don't meet any men I find attractive. Then I remind her of the years of unhappiness she had with my father. I think to myself, is it really worth all the turmoil and pain? It sure doesn't seem so right now. I told my equally inquisitive sister that I'm happy being alone so she'll stop trying to set me up with another one of her lame friends. At the last family gathering I told everyone I was super busy at work, no time for a boyfriend.

I tell my friends that I'm too old for a serious love relationship. Time has passed me by, and I don't want to deal with another person's baggage or drama. It's too much hard work and compromise. I'd never get to do what I really want to do again without someone else interfering or having input. I'm just not willing to do that anymore. Most of my friends have heard my dating horror stories and know I'm far too picky to settle. There are way too many creeps out there.

Now comes the hard part – what I tell myself. I just haven't found the right guy. All of the good ones seem to be taken. Most men don't want a strong, confident, successful woman. I'll have to "dumb myself down" or cater to them. When I really tune into my "gut" feelings, I realize I don't think I'm worthy of true love. Even if it comes my way, I don't trust myself not to mess it up. I don't think I can handle getting my heart broken again. I'm afraid to be vulnerable – it might hurt too much.

Exercise 4: Go through your story using a highlighter to mark each of the limiting beliefs you included. Write them down on a separate sheet of paper. Review your list and include anything else you think about men, love, dating, and marriage that resonates with you, even if it is not included in your story. Take time to make your list as comprehensive as possible.

Example:

- I'm not attracted to any of the men I meet
- I'm happy being alone
- I'm too busy to have a boyfriend
- Marriage is too much hard work
- I'm too old to fall in love
- Most men come with too much baggage
- Most men fall into the "creeps" category
- Love requires too many compromises
- Men don't want strong, confident women like me
- All the good men are taken
- No one meets my standards
- I'm not really worthy of true love
- I'll get my heart broken
- Love always hurts

Note: Let your list sit for a few days before going onto the next exercise.

Exercise 5: Look at your list of beliefs. You may notice that you've written them in the present tense. You did this without thinking about it because these are your current beliefs. In order to change your outcome, I'm going to help you subtly shift these beliefs out of the present and into the past where they belong. Don't worry; you don't have to struggle with this exercise. Just follow the instructions and gently let the beliefs fade into your past. On a new sheet of paper re-write your beliefs in the past tense. Begin to think of them in this new way each time one of them pops into your head. This takes time and practice. Be gentle with yourself.

Example:

- I wasn't attracted to any of the men I met
- I thought I was happy being alone
- I was too busy to have a boyfriend
- I thought marriage was too much hard work
- I previously thought I was too old to fall in love
- I thought most men came with too much baggage
- Most men fell into the "creeps" category
- Love required too many compromises
- I previously thought men didn't want strong, confident women like me
- All the good men were taken
- No one met my standards
- I thought I wasn't worthy of true love
- I feared my heart would be broken
- I believed love always hurt

Exercise 6: Put your new list of past beliefs away. You don't need to think about them anymore. From time to time one or more of your past beliefs will come to mind. When that happens gently remind yourself that you no longer think this way, but now you are open to new more productive beliefs. Simply repeat the belief again, reframing it in past tense.

Chapter Ten

Think About It

Marcelle and I met our freshman year in college, quickly becoming best friends. Boston was a new experience for me, having been raised in a small town in West Virginia, but I loved every minute of it. Marcelle, a lovely exotic name I thought, was from one of Boston's surrounding towns. She knew the city well. I was thrilled to be in college in a big city visiting museums, attending concerts at the Symphony, and riding the subway for the first time in my life. During our free time, Marcelle and I talked for hours on end, most often about men and dating. Looking back, I'm amused by our passionate lengthy conversations and dedication to the details on dressing for dating success.

Planning a date night out took on a life of its own. It became a project of such proportions you might think we were planning a Governor's Ball. No detail was left to chance regarding the all-important decision of what we were going to wear. We must have thought it could make or break our romantic futures should we choose the wrong anything for our date night.

Each item we planned to wear was carefully selected, then tried on for hours, adjusting absolutely everything that would grace our bodies, including undergarments – matching of course. By the time we finished our preparations, we had most of our clothes, shoes, belts, scarves etc. strewn everywhere. We thought it all through and didn't stop until we were completely satisfied we had the perfect outfit. This happened so often that after a particularly long session, Marcelle said with a long sigh, "This is like an act of Congress." From that point on we'd call each other and say, "It's time for an "act of Congress; I have a date this weekend."

When I recalled this story, it reminded me that it's possible to spend too much time thinking about things that don't really matter in the big scheme of life. We were young, both good students, so this overzealous thinking on our part was harmless fun and part of our process of maturing. The "acts of Congress" became fewer and shorter. As our interests developed with our maturity, we learned that dating was about more than the perfect outfit.

Not everything in life needs to be an "act of Congress." Some things need serious thought, others not so much. It is possible to over-think oneself into a state of paralysis and never get anything done. It is also possible to disregard the need to think about something important in order to make an informed choice or decision.

When women don't put any thought into the kind of partner they really want in their lives, they give up their right to choose. Leaving such an important life choice to serendipity may not yield the best results. Will it really matter if you spent hours primping and looking your best just to spend the evening with Mr. Wrong? Even nice guys can turn out to be poor matches for you. Dating can be fun. You can meet interesting people, but that doesn't mean they're destined to become long-term relationships.

During your recess from the search, consider taking time to think about what you really want in a life partner. Who is the person you want to share an intimate relationship with? Tap into the categories of intimacy from the previous section to determine who that ideal person is spiritually, physically, emotionally, and intellectually. Make a list about your true desires and begin to establish the standards you want to inform your choices.

Set aside time for yourself alone to relax and allow your inner guidance to direct your thinking. Make a cup of tea, put on comfortable clothes, and sit in a space where you can breathe and tune in to all of your senses. Allow the essence of your special someone to emerge. Don't make this exercise hard by analyzing everything that comes to mind. That only serves to create tension. Jot down everything without editing. You can always modify the list later. This is a positive way to use the *Law of Attraction*. Tune into your heart, and remember you can't get it wrong if you listen to your intuition.

Using the four types of intimacy you've already read about in this book, carefully consider each one and begin to make your list. In the pages that follow I've given you examples from my own life to help you get started. Compile your list only after you are relaxed and prepared to listen to your own intuition, thoughts and feelings. Just remember that you can re-visit your list anytime to make any changes should you so desire. Be thoughtful with this exercise, but have fun with it as well!

Spiritual Intimacy

Spiritual intimacy, once lacking, became a priority for me when I thought about my life partner. It became the first thing on my list. I wanted someone in my life who believed in a *Creator* and in our fellow human beings as part of the divine creation. It wasn't necessary for us to have the same religious beliefs or traditions. However, my desire was to be in a space of awareness with my partner for mutual sharing – without judgment.

Rather than require total agreement in our beliefs, I wanted a life partner to walk with me on my spiritual journey, willing to learn and grow. Being able to talk openly and explore our thoughts on spiritual matters may seem like an obvious expectation of marriage; but when it's missing, the absence can drain your energy and negatively affect your life in many ways.

Spend time thinking about the spiritual aspects of your own life and how you see them manifesting in your choice of relationships. Don't be tempted to think you can meet someone and then "convert" him to your beliefs once he has fallen madly in love with you. That's not fair and it can be detrimental. Besides, this time is for you to get really clear on what you want the *Universe* to co-create with you, not what you want to change about someone else. Lasting change only happens willingly from within. Change demanded isn't likely to last, if it happens at all.

Many years ago I didn't understand the importance of being clear on the values and characteristics I wanted in a husband. No one suggested making a list. I've come to understand with my mistakes how important the list is. When reflecting on the relationship I now share with my husband, it became clear - the list was written on my heart.

My husband is the manifestation of my heart's desire for a spiritually conscious man. He recognizes the beauty and majesty of all of creation and the divinity of all people, the daily translation of which I love. For example, I know he deeply respects me and all others with whom he connects in daily life. That makes my life more pleasant. Because of his respect for the planet, we live more "green" as partners. The spiritual compatibility we share is part of balancing the relationship scale to the side of that easy flowing pleasurable and satisfying life I so desired.

Your list will be unique to your needs and wants. Making spirituality part of your list may also be the opportunity to think more fully about your own spirituality. It's okay not to know exactly what your spiritual beliefs are. Spirituality may not have been part of your history; and even if it was, you may still be formulating your own beliefs. Continue to do so. Think about it and decide for yourself by reading, exploring, and talking with others to form your own understanding.

Knowing where you stand on spiritual matters not only benefits you, but also creates a cohesive understanding with your partner. Spirituality differences have the potential to cause enormous strife. Clarity about your lifestyle choices creates the energy necessary to attract someone compatible.

When children become part of a marriage, the need to know your partner's beliefs and wishes increases tenfold. Parenting issues are bound to surface. Knowing each other's spiritual thoughts, beliefs, and desires early in the relationship will help when the necessary discussions begin. Deciding on a spiritual direction for your family after the children have arrived can cause unwanted chaos. Consider what spiritual characteristics you are looking for in a life partner and add them to your list.

Physical Intimacy

Physical intimacy is a special bond we expect to have with our partner and we want the chemistry to be wonderful. It would seem alignment on this type of intimacy would come naturally, too obvious to have to think about. After all, from the time we first meet, physical appearance plays a significant role in our attraction. Without a physical attraction, physical intimacy would be difficult to develop and sustain. For many women, this is where the story goes off track.

We assume too much about our own physical attractiveness and assume we know more than we do about our date. Just because he's drop dead gorgeous, doesn't mean he's a great catch or a great match for you. Just because you look fabulous, doesn't mean every guy you meet will fall for you. Over-reliance on physical attraction can be a recipe for disaster in a love relationship. Physical attraction is important, even essential. So you will want to include it on your list.

Envisioning the ideal tall, muscular, handsome man of your dreams may make you smile, but that's not the only thing you need to consider about physical intimacy. Health and activity compatibility are important considerations. While the color of his hair, his skin, his eyes, may be alluring, looking into those eyes to what's really inside is equally vital.

Whether he's short, tall, round, lean, gorgeous, average, or plain; in the end, none of it will matter if his health can't sustain his appearance. We've been bombarded by idealized images of the perfect bodies and faces. It may be challenging not to think about these models and add them to our list. I encourage you to resist this temptation. The appearance factor is very real. However, unlike the animal kingdom where looks, smell, singing, and/or dancing abilities take priority, we have more to consider.

Spending my time with someone who cared about his health was on my list. This included someone who wanted to eat a healthy diet, someone who wanted to take walks with me, and someone who was generally physically fit. Partnering with a smoker was a definite "no." I didn't want to be married to a couch potato either. I wanted a healthy, active husband who enjoyed the outdoors and a man with whom there was sexual compatibility.

When you are thinking about this part of your list, be careful not to get side-tracked in the idealized world of perfection that requires you and your partner to be mirror images of one another. For example, my husband is a certified scuba dive master. I don't join him in that activity because I don't feel comfortable putting my face under water. He knows how I feel and doesn't insist that I try it anyway. He can scuba dive with friends or with his children while I read a book on the beach or relax on the boat. We don't plan our vacations around diving, so that arrangement works for us. Others feel differently and want their life partners to enjoy all their hobbies. What's most important is to find a balance that works for you.

I wanted someone who enjoys grocery shopping and cooking. We love to sit over tea on Saturday morning after breakfast and plan our menu for the week. We miss our little ritual when one of us is out of town. Weekend cooking with a glass of wine and great conversation brings us joy and creates that bond of physical intimacy we both really wanted. We share a strong need for physical affection often holding hands, sitting close to each other, hugging and kissing frequently, etc. The etcetera I'll leave to your imagination – let's just say we have terrific compatibility in the physical intimacy department.

I didn't plan that consciously, but I did have thoughts about exactly those things. My co-creation with the *Universe* manifested beyond any expectation I could have imagined. What may not have been clear in my mind was most assuredly clear in my heart. I encourage you to make your conscious choices by thinking about what you really want and including it on your list. It is much easier to visualize what you want when you get clarity regarding your choices. If you are a warm, affectionate person who loves the physicality of intimacy on all levels, you won't want to settle for someone who doesn't enjoy being touched outside of the bedroom.

Emotional Intimacy

Emotional Intimacy is a scary thought for some people. The word emotion challenges many people, especially men. It's what I missed the most in my first marriage. I didn't know it then; but once it came into my life, I knew I didn't want to be without it. I'm sure emotional intimacy means different things for different people, so I'll share what it meant for me and what some of the things were on my list.

I wanted to feel that someone cared about what I was thinking and feeling. I wanted my presence in his life to make a difference – a positive impactful difference. I wanted to be welcomed home at the end of the day or from a business trip with a smile and a hug. I wanted to be with someone who preferred my company to my absence. I wanted support for my bad day at work, support for having dealt with a jackass who hurt my feelings. Notice I said support, not unsolicited advice about what I should or shouldn't have done.

I wanted my husband to go out with me and feel proud to introduce me as his wife. I wanted a husband who was tuned in enough to my feelings and my presence that he might notice I was wearing a new dress or had my hair cut – at least most of the time. I wanted to know for sure I could ask for a hug, a smile, a kiss, support without any thought of rejection. I wanted someone who cared about my happiness as much as I cared about his. I didn't expect him to be clairvoyant and know my every need without having to ask. That would be nice, but it also robs us of that air of mystery. Think about what your needs are for emotional intimacy in a love relationship and add them to your list.

Intellectual Intimacy

Intellectual intimacy may be something most of us don't think much about. It may be assumed because the lack of intellectual compatibility usually prevents the dating relationship from progressing to the next stage. But I do think it is important to stop and consider what you want in this area. One of the women interviewed put it quite succinctly when she told me, "I want someone in my own reading group." She'd become clear about her need in this area after some less than intellectually satisfying dates.

Wanting a comfortable flow of dialogue on a variety of subjects with your partner is not snobbish – it's an authentic desire for compatibility. You both have areas of expertise to add to the conversation. Hopefully that will create a continual, positive learning environment for each other. Being able to discuss your life, your career, your beliefs, your understanding of an issue is one of the rewarding benefits of being in a marriage or long-term partnership.

During the book interviews, I often heard about intellectual condescension in relationships. The women didn't exactly put it that way, but they definitely felt the disconnection when it was happening to them. The degree of condescension ranged from subtle to abusive.

If a person doesn't know something, it doesn't mean he/she is stupid. It's merely reflective of his/her experience and/or education. We are all here to learn, and we're all at different stages of learning.

Great partnerships celebrate each other's intellectual journeys and provide love and support.

I love to hear about new things my husband has read about or studied. If he starts getting too technical, we joke about my eyes glazing over or I laugh and let him know that's enough of the details. The same thing happens when the roles are reversed. Your desire for intellectual intimacy will be unique to you and your partner as are all areas of intimacy.

My husband and I have similar levels of business and volunteer leadership experience, education levels, and general interests. That's what works for us. Think about what it will take for you and your mate to have lifelong pleasure in each other's company talking, laughing, and learning.

Once you've completed your list, based on the four types of intimacy and your standards and values for your relationship, review it for clarity and completion. If it feels right, that's great. You can add anything you think may be needed at any time. Once you're satisfied, put it away. Any tension around your list may only be detrimental to your purpose. Your list has set the *Law of Attraction* in motion, which alerted the *Universe* to your heart's desire. Feel the satisfaction and peace that comes with that type of clarity and support.

As you read the next story, carefully consider the value of making your list. Zoe had no idea that her friend's gentle insistence on making a list would turn out to be so prophetic. Her story has a fairytale ending, but it came very close to being a tragedy in every sense of the word.

"Much to my surprise, this man possessed every quality I'd written on my list two years earlier and none of the things I didn't want."

Zoe

Zoe's Story

Tall, thin, blonde, and blue-eyed was the package Zoe thought her true love would arrive in since that was what usually caught her attention. The night she met Jim, he nearly sat on her – literally. She was new in town, and Shana, a co-worker, invited her to a local singles hot spot. Zoe was excited to go since she didn't really know anyone there yet.

They sat in a booth in the corner. One of Shana's male friends came over to talk, taking a seat beside Shana. Jim saw them from across the room. Knowing Shana's friend, he decided to come over and say hello. He hadn't noticed Zoe sitting there. Without looking, he slid into the booth next to her, almost sitting in her lap. The four of them talked for hours. Zoe didn't think too much about their encounter because Jim looked nothing like the guys she usually dated. He was quite muscular and had dark hair and eyes.

For the next two weeks she was out of town, but Jim called her as soon as she returned. They went out for dinner and talked for hours, late into the night. He dropped her off at the hotel where she was temporarily living, and they had their first kiss. It was hard to stop.

This was not supposed to be happening. Zoe was not looking for a man. She'd been in a three year romantic relationship right out of college which had become physically threatening. The man took control early in the relationship, changing the way Zoe related to herself, her friends, and family. This relationship ended badly with a court battle and threats of physical harm, including an incident where he attempted to run her off the road. In addition, he sent her a note while she was in a restaurant telling her he had a "thirty-eight special" for her. She went straight to the police. She was so frightened of him, she moved to the other side of the city, far away from his family and their friends.

Sometime later, a friend encouraged Zoe to make a list of all the positive characteristics she was looking for in a partner and to think about what she didn't want. She decided to do it. She made her list and put it away in a dresser drawer.

Zoe had worked all day at a trade show booth with medical professionals wearing a hat and surgical mask most of the time. Jim had planned to meet her there to take her to dinner. Zoe remembers thinking about how dreadful she must have looked that evening with no time to freshen up and re-apply makeup or re-arrange her flat hair. She looked up and saw him coming toward her in a suit with the sun hitting his face. That's when she saw him for the first time – completely. She was taken aback by how handsome he was. Until that moment, she hadn't really noticed his physical appearance. However, she certainly took notice of the connection she felt with him that night.

He asked her to join him for the weekend with a few friends in a cabin in the mountains. She readily agreed, not having seen much of this new state she was now living in. They had planned to leave after work on Friday, but Zoe could not get away. In fact, she wasn't finished with her work until 2 a.m. When she called Jim to let him know, he suggested an early Saturday morning departure instead. When they arrived at the cabin, Zoe happily realized there were no other friends coming. They had a great time going out to dinner, talking for hours, and dancing.

That Monday, he'd purchased tickets for a Stevie Ray Vaughn concert. At the concert, Jim told Zoe he loved her. She was thrilled to tell him she felt the same way. However, she was happy and mad about it at the same time. The reason she was in Jim's city was because she had been training for what she called "the best job in the industry" – a pacemaker sales representative position. Unfortunately, her dream job was actually in El Paso, Texas. She'd set clear intentions to focus on her career, which meant no love connection for now.

She finished the training and returned to El Paso with the plan to visit Jim every two weeks. That schedule lasted for three months before they decided a long distance romance was not what they wanted. Zoe left her dream job and moved to be with Jim. When she was packing her belongings for the move, she found "the list." She sat down to read it and was amazed. Jim had all of the positive characteristics she'd put on her list and none of the negatives. She sent him the list letting him know it had been written almost two years before they met. They've been married now for seventeen years and have two children. Her eyes sparkle brightly when recounting their love story.

LOVE COACHING PROGRAM

It's ALL About YOU

PERSONAL PLANNER

STEP TWO: **Think About It** (Making Your List)

As you've just read in this chapter, it's vital to spend time thinking about what you want in a love relationship, what values and characteristics you desire in your mate, and what you bring to the relationship as well. This is the second step in the love coaching process. Take time to reflect on your heart's desires and complete the exercises below. They are designed to keep you moving forward on the path to finding your love connection while gently nudging you to shift your previous beliefs behaviors and experiences.

Exercise 1: Continue your daily Gratitude practice. Now that you've worked with the letters of your name, you can shift to writing about your gratitude for the objects you value in your environment. As you look around each day, try to list something different. Read each night before going to bed.

Example:

- ♡ I'm grateful for my warm, soft bed
- ♡ I love my reliable car
- ♡ I appreciate the beauty of my backyard
- ♡ I'm grateful for my nice, quiet neighborhood
- ♡ I'm grateful for the beautiful scarf I wore today
- ♡ I so appreciate the warmth of the sun
- ♡ I love the beauty of the snow
- ♡ I'm grateful for the snow plows
- ♡ I'm grateful for my warm home

Exercise 2: As you read earlier in this chapter, it's important to find a comfortable environment and have plenty of time to begin this next exercise. Now it's time to think about making your personal detailed list. To help you customize your list you'll want to review the following examples, thinking about what resonates with you. Remember, these are only examples. Your list needs to make sense to you. Feel free to list whatever comes to your mind in each category. You'll edit the list later.

Note: Don't be tempted to write a novel – choose only those attributes you deeply value and leave the details to the *Universal Creative Energy Source.*

Physical Attributes Example:

- ♡ Loves to exercise and stay fit
- ♡ Has a warm smile
- ♡ Is a generous lover
- ♡ Takes pride in his appearance
- ♡ We're sexually compatible
- ♡ Maintains a healthy weight
- ♡ Enjoys outdoor activities
- ♡ Gives great hugs

Emotional Attributes Example:

- ♡ Expresses emotions in healthy ways
- ♡ Has a great sense of humor
- ♡ Can laugh and cry with me
- ♡ Has a positive attitude about life
- ♡ Supports me publicly and privately
- ♡ Handles conflict well
- ♡ Shows interest in my feelings and ideas
- ♡ Is generous and kind
- ♡ Displays empathy for others

Intellectual Attributes Example:

- ♡ Respects my viewpoint
- ♡ Is willing to change his mind
- ♡ Likes to read and learn
- ♡ Values education
- ♡ Readily seeks my advice
- ♡ Is willing to admit mistakes
- ♡ Is an interesting conversationalist
- ♡ Can discuss world affairs
- ♡ Has outside interests

Spiritual Attributes Example:

- ♡ Believes in a higher power
- ♡ Has a kind and generous heart
- ♡ Has an attitude of gratitude
- ♡ Demonstrates strong core values
- ♡ Respects other's religious beliefs
- ♡ Takes responsibility for his own life
- ♡ Is trustworthy
- ♡ Cares about the planet
- ♡ Shows compassion for others
- ♡ Willing to participate in charitable giving
- ♡ Loves animals

Exercise 3: Spend time with your list and decide on your true priorities. I encourage you to limit your list to the top 20 – 25 attributes. Having a lengthy list is not necessary to solidify your ideal mate's characteristics. Once you've completed a list with which you are comfortable, read it aloud. Then feel the amazing possibilities, bless it with a kiss, and fold it up and put it away. Do not obsess over it. Know in your heart the *Universe* has heard your deepest desires. Relax – you can always add to it later, if you feel you've forgotten something important. Breathe, relax, breathe, relax and repeat.

Chapter Eleven

Just Do It

Now that you've been on recess from the search and made your list, it's time to take action. The first step put a stop to struggle; the second step brought clarity and self-reflection; this third step is a call to action. Taking action does not require "an act of Congress." You've probably already thought about some of what you're about to read – maybe a little too much if it' has paralyzed you into inaction. You'll know if you need to make changes in any of the areas covered in this chapter.

You may need someone to give you a nudge in the direction of right action. This chapter is focused on moving from thinking to doing. Years ago, one of my dear, funny, extroverted girlfriends did that for me. I didn't like it at the time, but I'm grateful that it happened. It was the push I needed to move ahead with creating the life I desired.

I'm sure I complained more than a few times that I needed to lose a few pounds. One day, she looked me straight in the eyes and said, "Why don't you stop talking about it and just do it." That wasn't the support I had in mind. I expected some friendly commiseration on the topic, not a straightforward, "get off your backside and get on with it" message. Adding insult to injury, she obviously thought I needed to lose a few pounds as well.

Although not delighted by her comment, it made me stop and re-evaluate my weight situation. Her direct comment served to open my eyes to the facts. I was twenty-five pounds overweight and unhappy about it; yet I hadn't managed to do anything to change it. No extraordinary resources or research were needed, just a jolt into reality and a decision to take action.

It's not complicated for most of us to lose some weight. All we need to do is eat the right foods in moderate amounts and exercise. Replace bad choices with good ones. That's simple. I decided to stop thinking about it and just do it. I lost the weight, felt great, and thanked my friend for the kick start.

This chapter is your gentle nudge to "fix" those things you've thought about a hundred times. Change the things you want because you want to, not because someone else wants you to. You have time to do this since you're still on recess and your list has been made and put away. Right now, it's all about you. What do you want to do for yourself? What do you want to stop giving energy to so you can show up for life as your best self? I've listed some areas for consideration. If they fit, don't think about them for long; just make a decision and take action. Change emerges one step at a time. Decide to put one foot forward to begin.

If you need to lose weight to be your healthiest, decide to start now – today. Just do it with real food, real exercise, and real concern for being healthy without trying to be a certain size. There are many resources to help you if you want assistance. You can start by replacing one bad habit at a time with a good one. For example, give up soda and replace it with water and green tea. Going on and off special diets doesn't address the real issue. The real key to maintaining a healthy weight is adopting a healthier lifestyle. If you believe you can do it, then you can.

If you look in the mirror and don't like what you see, it's time for a change. If it's your hair, make an appointment with a good hairdresser (probably not your current one) and ask for advice. If you know someone who has a fabulous haircut and color, ask her for a recommendation. You can also ask a friend for an honest assessment.

If you want to take better care of your skin and need direction, ask someone who has healthy, great looking skin. Department store skin care sales people are knowledgeable resources as well. Looking your best will make you feel more confident. Confidence is ranked high on the list of sexy characteristics, according to many men.

Feeling frumpy or wearing clothes that aren't truly reflective of who you are is an easy fix. If you need help, ask a well-dressed friend or make an appointment with a retail store personal shopper. Sometimes it's not the clothes themselves, but the poor fit or an unflattering combination of pieces. Looking fabulous doesn't have to cost a lot of money. Look for quality pieces at sale or clearance prices. You may be able to use what you already own with a little tailoring or accessorizing. It's all about feeling terrific in your clothes. So don't wear things you don't like just to please someone else.

This is a great time to try something different, perhaps a newer style you may not have ever considered. You may want a more updated look; but if you don't, it's okay. Only buy clothes you truly love and ones that make you feel like a million dollars.

The point of this make-over is for you to be able to look in the mirror every day and smile, knowing you look your best. It's not about getting you to do anything you don't want to do. If you prefer the no make-up fresh face look, by all means, flaunt your healthy looking skin. If you don't want to color your hair, get a style that works for you to be your personal best. Whatever you do, make sure you can look in the mirror and say with confidence, "I am healthy and look fabulous today."

I am addressing the externals first, not because they're most important, but because they're something tangible to start with before tackling more challenging projects. Spending any time thinking about how unhappy we are with our appearance takes energy away from the more important things in life. If that is something you want to change, decide to stop dwelling on it and just do it. You'll feel more confident when you know you are looking fine.

Next, look at your home or apartment. Is there unnecessary clutter? Is it a dirty mess? Does your garage contain everything but your car? Is house cleaning a four letter word? Living surrounded by things you don't need or use creates negative energy that inadvertently affects your life. Instead of finding excuses to put off today what you probably will not do tomorrow, start with something small. Take one step at a time or one room at a time. You'll be surprised at how quickly things start to reflect real change. If you need help, ask a friend to assist in exchange for something she need from you. You could create a date with a friend to de-clutter and clean each other's homes together if you can't face it alone.

Your home, whether large or small, should be a sanctuary for your enjoyment and relaxation. If you've created that type of environment; you are many steps ahead. If not, you probably realize your environment is the opposite of relaxing and welcoming. Suggesting this change is about removing the negative energy in your space and replacing it with the positive energy that comes from knowing you've created a retreat for yourself. You can find things when you need them and you can clean more quickly with clutter eliminated.

This is an important aspect of living life more fully. How large or small a task it is depends on how well you manage it. When I put off something I know I need to do, the energy I expend thinking about it is always more draining than just doing it. It never takes as long as I've imagined it will and I often end up feeling silly for delaying it so long. If you don't feel relaxed and happy in your home environment, make a plan for change and "just do it." Once these external manifestations are taken care of, you can turn your time and energy to other important aspects of life.

I digress momentarily to address a necessary point. Living with your opposite in terms of neatness and cleanliness is challenging and will wear you down. I've witnessed mismatches in this area, and I have seen the results of frustrated angry spouses. It's okay to overlook small differences and compromise once in a while, but constantly picking up after an untidy person can fuel resentment.

If you've taken the time and put in the effort to look your personal best, you'll want your home to reflect that as well. It's far easier to keep an uncluttered home clean and in order than to routinely find yourself doing major overhaul projects due to bad habits.

When you are happy with how you look and feel and how your house looks and feels, you'll attract like energies into your space. This may feel like small stuff in comparison to internal issues. However, when unchecked, it can grow to monumental proportions. That's why I've suggested handling it first. That's especially important if any of these things were already on your list of things to do someday.

Your state of relaxation and happiness matters in the co-creation process. Being unhappy with your body, your health, and/or your home increases the negative energy which can block the good you want to have in your life. A cluttered home indicates cluttered thinking. As you know by now, thinking clearly is essential for developing the standards you'll set for yourself and for what you will accept in a love partnership. Move from thinking about the changes you want to make to implementing them in order to move ahead with feeling more joy.

I've spent most of this chapter talking about externals to set a foundation for pursuing the all-important and rewarding internal journey. It's still all about you. You must find your own center of joy and step fully into who you are. It's up to you to discover and honor yourself. That's an essential beginning to sharing life with someone else. If you desire a happy, healthy partner who takes care of himself and his possessions, you need to have those qualities as well. You cannot share what you do not have, and you cannot attract that which you are blocking.

You've made a list of the qualities you're looking for in a partner. Do you have those same qualities? If you want someone to speak kindly to you, are your words kind; or are they harsh and often judgmental? If you want a partner with integrity, do you walk with integrity in your daily life? If you prefer to be in the company of joyful, optimistic people, are you projecting the same? If you want a partner with compassion for others and a generous spirit, are you practicing compassion and generosity?

When we have become those very things we are looking for in our mate, we'll easily recognize them more readily in others. It's necessary to evaluate your own "essential nature" and begin to change anything that is incongruent with your values. Expecting to receive what you are unwilling to give is a one-sided proposition. Successful relationships have a strong measure of balance. They are not tipped heavily in favor of one partner. Your behavior must mirror what you want.

We all know we aren't going to be thinner unless we do something to make it happen. Making internal changes works the same way and takes time. Deciding to be a calmer, more centered person starts with making the decision to do so, but it will only happen with the practice of behaving calmly when it would be easier not to do so. Sometimes we get so focused on reading the recipe, we forget to take action. If you want a chocolate cake for dessert, you not only have to read the recipe, you also must mix the ingredients and bake the cake. The decision precedes the action, but it does not stand alone. If the results aren't perfect the first time, keep practicing.

When my husband and I decided we wanted to stop carrying home so many plastic shopping bags, it took a while to develop a better habit. Sometimes we forgot the reusable bags, leaving them at home, or we left them in the car instead of bringing them into the store. With practice, it became a habit we don't forget. We didn't berate ourselves for mistakes; we kept our resolve to make the change. By putting the bags back in the car after using them, we accomplished our goal. Now the bags are always there, even if we forget and have to leave the store momentarily to retrieve them.

It's important to find a practice that works for you. There is no shortage of self-help books to assist you. Self-reflection, meditation, affirmations, visualization, reading, support groups, and any number of reminders from bracelets to cards in your pocket can be effective for assisting you in facilitating the changes you want to make. By all means, relax. Have some fun in the process. Remember, it is a process. Above all, decide what you want to change for yourself – not for anyone else – and just do it.

The story you'll read next is from a woman who needed to change a number of things in her life that weren't working. The love of her life wasn't to be until she was ready to recognize the truth of her circumstances and take the necessary action to move forward.

Marian was singularly focused on her appearance and the appearance of her boyfriends – so much so that she kept right on doing the same things and expecting different results. Some say that is the definition of insanity. I say it's just one of the all too human traps we fall into until we wake up and open our eyes to what we've been doing and thinking. When we finally awaken, it's like someone flipped on a light switch in a darkened room – one in which we've been sleep-walking. It can be a hard lesson to realize that we kept trying the same things, over and over, thinking the outcome would change.

Consider Marian's story if you're experiencing undesirable results from what you've been doing, especially if you've been denying the reality that something needs to change. Being aware of the need to change something is an important place to begin; however, nothing really changes without action.

We all know change is necessary, but it's often easier to think about than to do. Think about this story in terms of your life, and decide to take action in any area that isn't working for you. Marian didn't have weight or general appearance issues, or did she? You may be surprised at what she actually needed to address and change. I'm sure you won't be surprised at the outcome of her decisions.

"I stayed in relationships for years that should have lasted only five minutes. Had my self-esteem been more fragile….I might have married them too."

Marian

Marian's Story

"Oh my God, what was I thinking?" was one of the first things Marian said to me in our interview. She described herself as a serial relationship person from the age of sixteen to thirty-six. From her earliest memories, Marian was admired and rewarded for being pretty, which developed her sense that personal appearance was highly prized by everyone. She could not recall ever being told she was smart, talented, kind, generous, or anything other than pretty. In hindsight, she realized this sentiment, although well intentioned, must have planted a seed that internalized the high value of physical appearance and its importance relative to other characteristics.

Marian dated many handsome losers, especially in her twenties, thinking she was expected to be with someone equally attractive. The man in her life was a reflection of who she thought she was, so dating anyone she didn't think was physically attractive was unthinkable. For her, that value was so strong it eclipsed all other considerations. The results were disastrous for Marian.

Her laser-like focus on appearance attracted men without many other redeeming qualities. Marian's boyfriends were often emotionally unavailable with a host of personal problems, including drug and alcohol addictions. She overlooked their "minor" problems because they were handsome and looked quite fine by her side. The tape running in her head since childhood was to look good and be with someone who looked equally as well as she did. With such a foundational belief, Marian dismissed the addictions and the verbal abuse which permeated her daily existence. Things went from bad to worse before Marian's wake up call.

Her last boyfriend was a tall, muscular, handsome, professional basketball player with passive-aggressive behaviors. Like the other men in her life, he was emotionally unavailable. In addition, he had sexual addiction problems. She knew he was not the one for her, but she kept trying to "fix" him anyway. All of her other boyfriends had been "fix-it projects," and this one was no exception. Although she never managed to completely "fix" her men, that didn't stop her from repeatedly trying to improve him – for almost two decades.

One particular night after they'd been dating for nine months, a red flag suddenly appeared when he introduced her as his "friend." Marian was dumbfounded. Still she held on, in spite of knowing the relationship had already suffered that fatal blow. When she couldn't walk away, he did.

It took a massive storm of five feet of snow for Marian to get it. Stranded in her apartment for three days provided the space for her own personal avalanche and subsequent impetus to dig out. Three days in a small apartment with the roommate from hell was a good beginning. While thinking about her job, which she hated, she received the farewell email from the basketball player. Although nicely done, it was still an email. The break-up was not unexpected, but an email was the final indignity. "Really, who does that?" she said. Intellectually, she'd known for a long time it wasn't the right relationship. The more she thought about him, the more she realized how irritating he was. Even the sound of his breathing had been annoying.

The snowstorm had become a metaphor for her life. One issue at a time accumulating to critical mass – the chatterbox roommate had driven her crazy, the pseudo boyfriend demeaned her very existence, and the job with no future, for which she felt no passion all crashed down in one moment. Suddenly, her whole perspective shifted. Something snapped that day, and Marian woke up for the first time in many years. She was thirty-five years old and decided everything in her life had to change. She vowed to have no more bad boyfriends, no more bad roommates, and no more bad jobs.

For the next year, Marian made a conscious decision not to date anyone. Instead, she looked for a new career – one she could fully embrace and enjoy. She had no idea what that would be, but she did know she wanted to be in control of how she spent her time and energy.

The relationship decision Marian made that day changed her life in a way she never expected. Her decision to take care of herself raised her expectations for a partner. She learned how to be content with herself and focus on her needs. In the absence of the energy sucking relationships she'd had in the past, she had time to think about what she wanted. As a result, she decided if someone wanted to share her life, he would have to meet her on her terms and be pretty amazing too. His appearance moved to the bottom of her priority list.

Sometime later, she ran into an old friend who wanted to talk and perhaps get together for lunch. Marian didn't respond. After the third contact, she relented and returned the call. Her friend was excited about her new career and invited her to a complimentary seminar. Since the topic intrigued Marian, she decided to go. Her friend couldn't stop talking about one of the firm's executives, telling Marian how wonderful he was. At the time, Marian's only interest was in finding a new, rewarding career, not in learning how great the managers were in this company.

Marian stepped slowly into her new business venture. She started part-time, while she studied for the licensing requirements. She passed in record time. It was soon evident that this was her calling, and she moved into full-time work. Months went by and she gradually got to know Sam, the manager her friend had spoken of. Although his marriage had ended, he'd been in no hurry to date. Marian says, "Everyone knew we were going to be together before we did." The connection, once recognized by both parties, was undeniable. They've been together for ten years and married for the past eight. They now enjoy an intimate partnership together at work and at home.

Marian says Sam never disappointed her and never neglected to call. In fact, she never questioned whether they would get married. She is grateful something always stopped her from marrying any of her previous boyfriends.

"Sam knows all about my past relationships and disappointments. He's never voiced an ounce of judgment or jealousy – there's no need for that." Marian says they are connected on many levels, including knowing what each other is going to say. They're often able to finish each other's sentences. They share goals and work together on everything. There were no red flags in this relationship.

Before Sam came into Marion's life, she spent many holidays alone, lying to her friends and family about having other plans just to protect her image. Even though she was caught up in appearances, her self-esteem was strong enough to protect her from walking into undesirable marriages. She said, "I stayed in relationships for years that should have lasted only five minutes. Had my self-esteem been more fragile, I might have married them."

Marian is grateful for the snowstorm that triggered her personal avalanche. What she has now is unconditional and comfortable in ways she never experienced before. They truly love being and working together.

As our meeting ended, Marian told me something I really love and want to share with you. Marion and her husband meet weekly to talk about their life plans, their future goals, and their budget. They have full disclosure on all levels, financially and emotionally. They share life on the same page. Marian's happiness radiated across her lovely face as she talked about the love of her life.

I hope you'll be inspired to look at your life, determine what needs to be changed, and just do it. If you want a new you, take the first step. Get rid of what doesn't work in your life, whether it's your hair style, unhealthy habits, toxic friends, bad love relationships, unrewarding jobs, or anything else.

Showing up for your best life is not only important; but also possible, regardless of where you are now. You are not your circumstances. As you try on your best self, know you are preparing to welcome in the love of your life.

LOVE COACHING PROGRAM

It's ALL About YOU

PERSONAL PLANNER

STEP THREE: **Just Do It** (Taking Action)

Exercise 1: Continue your daily Gratitude practice. This time focus on writing about the people in your life for whom you're grateful. Be sure to include family, friends, acquaintances, co-workers, strangers, and even people you may not have met. Don't forget to be grateful for your own contributions. As you look around each day, try to list someone different. Read each night before going to bed.

Example:

- ♡ I'm grateful for my sweet supportive mother
- ♡ I'm grateful for my wise and caring father
- ♡ I so appreciate the patient clerk at the store
- ♡ I'm grateful for the person who plowed the snow
- ♡ I so appreciate my good friend for her advice
- ♡ I love my healthy green eyes
- ♡ I'm grateful for my wise doctor
- ♡ I'm grateful for our wonderful ministers
- ♡ I'm grateful for my loving, supportive children

Exercise 2: You just read a chapter about making time to clear any clutter and/or distracting items from your life. Now is the time to make your personal list. There were examples from my personal list included in the chapter, and below I've included a long list from my coaching clients. I call these life distractions "Energy Zappers." Because they take your otherwise happy state of being and drag it down so incrementally, you may not realize how far it's gone until you take action. Take time to consider what actions you are willing to take. Remember: these are examples.

Energy Zappers

1. Unhealthy weight
2. Hair style and/or color that doesn't suit me
3. Clothes that are uncomfortable
4. Clothes that are worn out
5. Clothes that are unflattering
6. Excessive clutter in my house
7. Excessive clutter in my garage
8. Excessive clutter in my office
9. An unkempt or neglected yard
10. Broken jewelry
11. Not having a place for everything I own
12. Not having important papers organized, updated and filed
13. Not having photographs organized and stored
14. Room(s) in my home in need of fresh paint
15. Disorganized, cluttered kitchen cabinets
16. Carpet in need of cleaning
17. Worn out shoes
18. Too many shoes I don't like or wear
19. A computer that's too slow
20. No workable office filing system
21. Friendships that make me uncomfortable
22. Not making enough time for friends
23. Creaky doors in my home
24. A dirty car
25. Things in need of repair on my car
26. Driving with unsafe tires
27. Worn out bed linens
28. Not having a will
29. Overeating anything
30. Failing to eat good quality foods
31. Failing to drink enough water
32. Addiction to soda
33. Excessive alcohol consumption
34. Unwanted telephone calls
35. Not taking time to meditate
36. Not taking time to be still and do nothing
37. Tolerating a partner who is not acting like a partner

38. Constant self-criticism
39. Under valuing my time
40. Over committing to activities
41. Feeling stress around family members
42. Stressing about the holidays
43. Buying gifts I can't afford
44. Not having sufficient savings
45. Not having a budget
46. Not sticking to my budget
47. Watching too much television
48. Watching negative news programs before bed
49. Not getting enough sleep
50. Feeling rushed every day
51. Being taken advantage of at work
52. Allowing co-workers to negatively impact my day
53. Allowing my boss to yell at me
54. Not finding a charity and giving my time and/or money
55. Having a job I hate
56. Not making enough money
57. Having revolving credit card balances
58. Buying things I don't need
59. Not finding ways to reduce, reuse, or recycle
60. Forgetting my reusable grocery bags
61. Not changing light bulbs to more energy efficient ones
62. Not having an energy audit of my home
63. Living in an environment that doesn't contribute to my enjoyment of life
64. Missing friends and family birthdays or anniversaries
65. Not taking time to enjoy family traditions
66. Participating in family traditions that no longer uplift me
67. Waiting until the last minute to do my income taxes (or anything else)
68. Allowing trivial things to upset me
69. Not scheduling health care appointments
70. Not preparing my car for winter
71. Dwelling on past mistakes or heartbreaks

Exercise 3: You may now have a very long personalized list. Please take time to prioritize your list and decide which item(s) to tackle first. There may be things on your list you want to do, but you may be unwilling or unable to fix them at this time. Shorten your list if the mere sight of it gives you anxiety. The point of this exercise is to help inspire you to action, not to overwhelm you with inaction. Once you pick an item or two and accomplish the desired action, you may be surprised at how your body energy is affected. Hint: There's little time to stew over your dating hiatus or status when you are busy shifting negative energy out and replacing it with positive action!

Remember: You are not taking action for the sake of taking action – you are shifting the way you feel about your life.

Chapter Twelve

Embrace It

Waiting for someone else to walk in and complete you isn't the best strategy for a happy life. Without exception, the women I interviewed let me know how one decision changed everything – the decision to let go of the struggle and embrace their own happiness.

Victoria had been afraid of raising her daughter alone; but once she let that go and relaxed into her authentic desires, everything she wanted came to be. Since looking for a life partner did not occupy her thoughts, she whole-heartedly embraced the challenges of developing a new business and her role as a single mother.

While this choice was not easy, Victoria had clarity around her need to thrive in an environment of integrity and peace. As a result, she found unexpected inner strength, power, and happiness. She learned to give these gifts to herself, to her daughter, to her family and friends, and finally to the love of her life. Because she didn't wait for Clark to rescue or complete her, her wholeness birthed an authentic ability to share life more fully with a partner.

Are you engaging in activities you really dislike searching for a mate?? If you really don't enjoy watching football games, ask yourself why you're spending time doing it. If you think it's a great way to meet men, you're right. It's a great way to meet men who love to watch football games. Many men don't want to do anything else during football season. If that's what you want, then that's great. If not, start spending your leisure time engaged in activities you find pleasurable or relaxing and let that feed your personal well-being.

When Kaitlin first told me she attended a weekend knitting retreat, I was intrigued to say the least. I wondered how that would fit into a love story. Kaitlin's love for knitting, importing beautiful yarns from Ireland, fed her soul and allowed her to spend her leisure time doing what she enjoyed. Pursuit of her interests opened the channels for the *Universe* to co-create her fondest wish for a life partner. She wasn't looking. It happened when she fully embraced her own life.

If you find yourself thinking, "How in the world am I supposed to be happy? I definitely want to have love in my life so that I can get married, or have a long-term committed relationship, but I don't have either, I'm alone." It's vital to stop giving energy to what you do not want. Focusing on what you don't have brings more of the same. There are many terrific books on this topic, and I recommend you read at least one of them.

The *Law of Attraction* is real. I invite you to be open to that possibility, even if you've never heard of it, haven't experienced it, or think it's nuts. It can't hurt to consider the possibility that it does exist. People didn't know anything about electricity until Thomas Edison figured out how to use it. Just because you can't see or feel it, doesn't mean it doesn't exist. There are many things we can't see, but they're still very real. The *Law of Attraction* or *Law of Cause and Effect* falls into that category.

If you believe there is no ideal partner for you, you've created a powerful force repelling the very love you want. Remember that you are on recess from the search in order to eliminate your stress and the accompanying disappointments. Until you can reframe what you're doing and thinking, you can't expect different results.

The list establishing your standards puts positive higher frequency energy around your true desires. Taking steps to rid your life of unwanted ideas, people, and things removes negative energy and creates the space for more positive energies. Hopefully you've taken many of these steps by now.

This chapter is about embracing your life as you envision it. It's important to do that even if you aren't yet where you want to be. Embracing your authentic self and stepping into your best life with forward momentum brings you ever closer to your heart's desires. That's true for anything you think about.

Like so many others, I had to learn that lesson the hard way, and it took many attempts. In the past, I gave energy to negative thoughts about my job. The result – I was invited to leave. I actually had to stop myself from laughing when it happened. I knew I was inviting my joblessness, but I could not stop myself anyway. In one breath, I'd express the frustration and unhappiness; and in the next breath, I'd try to undo the negativity by adding a half-hearted statement of gratitude for the paycheck. It didn't work. The *Law of Attraction* worked. Deeply felt emotions are never trumped by mere words.

Determine what brings you joy and embrace it fully. If you like steak, eat steak. If you like long walks in the woods, go for a walk. If you do not want to spend time watching ballgames, don't. Above all, be honest with everyone about your preferences, including yourself. Caveat: it's not okay to say you don't like activities you haven't tried. It's important to push yourself beyond your comfort zone at times.

My husband thought he had a serious dislike of asparagus until he tasted it freshly grilled. I had to do a little coaxing to get him to try it, but he's glad he did.

Much to my surprise, my daughter likes watching football games. When I asked her about it she said she did not enjoy the games until someone taught her more about the rules of play. She gave it a chance and now she's a fan.

As you reinvent yourself, don't be afraid to try new activities. Meeting new people increases the likelihood of encountering true love. Notice, I didn't say searching for true love. There is no searching on this plan, only embracing your life with enthusiasm and joy.

The next story has an unexpected twist regarding the concept of embracing your life now. As you read it, take note of how young Faun neglected to find her personal happiness before embarking on a marriage journey that would end unpleasantly. See how she's transformed by first embracing her own life.

"I needed time alone to find my happiness before sharing my life with someone else."

Faun

Faun's Story

Faun was raised in America's heartland where the wheat thrives and idyllic families flourish. Childhood was uneventful and pleasant for most of Faun's life until her father decided to have an affair with the mother of her best friend. It was her senior year in high school. The family came apart. The house was lost and Faun's mother, in despair, sent her off to a woman's college.

Although her mother had good intentions, college didn't work out. Faun's grades were deplorable and she flunked out rather quickly. Feeling lost and still upset over her father's irresponsible actions, she didn't know quite what to do. However, finding a job was a necessity.

After finding work, she met a man who hadn't even finished high school, and they promptly married. Her need for security overtook her better judgement. The warning signs were there, but Faun ignored them. They argued frequently and fought vehemently the night before their wedding. Faun felt intense stress on her wedding day rather than the bliss she'd always dreamed about. Yet, she felt obligated to go through with the ceremony because of the expense her mother had invested, though she could ill afford it.

Nine months later on the 4th of July they had their final argument. The incessant emotional abuse finally culminated when Faun threw a bungee cord at her husband in fury and shouted, "That's it; I'm out of here." Both family and friends supported her decision. They thought she needed time to find herself and would eventually return to the marriage. That was not to be.

The emotional abuse Faun suffered was worse than anyone outside the marriage knew. Though pretending to embrace Faun's friends and family, her husband attempted to distance her from them by making excuses to avoid family gatherings and activities. He destroyed a longtime friendship with her best friend and Maid of Honor by telling Faun her friend had tried to seduce him the night before their wedding. Instead of the beaming bride Faun always wanted to be on her wedding day, she felt numb.

After the divorce, Faun moved on with her life, still unsure of her love relationship future. She accepted a position with a large company in a support services management role. One of the men she worked with on a project for several months became a close friend. She came to see his true nature through the work he did leading a difficult downsizing project. She then developed great respect for his thoughtful handling of the delicate situation.

He had a reputation for dating younger women. On one occasion point, Faun even matched him with another woman for a dinner date. When that didn't work out as planned, he asked Faun to accompany him for an outing. He cooked dinner at his place and gently took time to get to know her. Before long they were dating, taking long walks and camping.

As a result of several marriages, he'd learned quite a bit about relationships, and he was concerned about Faun's lack of experience and self-awareness. He wisely realized she didn't know what made her happy outside of a love relationship. She was smitten. When he was transferred out of state, she wanted to move with him. He gently insisted she learn how to be comfortable with herself before committing to a long-term relationship.

That decision was hard for Faun to accept since being with him was the best feeling she'd ever experienced. "It was so wonderful." It took many months, but she finally understood what he was trying to convey. She needed to spend time alone and find her own center and measure of happiness before attempting to share her life with him.

They dated for a year before marrying in Faun's mother's house. The day was the polar opposite of her first wedding. She knew for sure, no doubts, only joy. She described her gratitude for this marriage as intense and immense. Her first husband loved to point out her every mistake and used the information to tell her she wasn't good enough for him. This time, she trusted herself, confident she needed no one's confirmation of her self-worth.

Another healing moment came when she completed a Dale Carnegie course as part of a work training program for her new company. After class she wept for hours, thinking of her younger self, ill-equipped to make good choices, fully realizing she'd had no tools for dealing with her first marriage. Because she didn't possess the knowledge to deal with the issues, her marriage had been a constant struggle. When her co-workers and manager sensed her lack of self-esteem, they offered assertiveness training. That training taught Faun to stand up to a powerful male in the company and ask, "Why do you always interrupt me when I am talking?"

Faun moved light years ahead in her self-awareness and confidence. Recently, she enjoyed an all-women's sailing trip to the Virgin Islands. When her husband spent a month in South America before she could join him, Faun had another opportunity to demonstrate her new found self-confidence. Upon her arrival the desk clerk made them both laugh out loud when she said, "Now you're complete." Faun replied, "No we're already complete. Our relationship is a bonus."

They genuinely liked each other and choose every day to be together. That relationship dynamic is a stark contrast to her first marriage. Faun said she later realized that her first husband didn't even like her, and actually she didn't like him. Now, instead of fighting and not caring what is said or how it's said, her marriage is based on integrity and genuine respect for each other. Any differences are settled with grace.

How will your life change by choosing to embrace your authentic self? Please take time to think about your choices and reflect on anything you might want to change and/or embrace.

When I read the following quote from Abraham Hicks, I knew it was a perfect summation for this Chapter, Embracing Your Life.

"If you let your dominant intention be to revise and improve the content of the story you tell every day of your life, it is our absolute promise to you that your life will become that ever-improving story. For the powerful *Law of Attraction* – the essence of that which is like unto itself is drawn – it must be!"

Learn to embrace this quote. Place it in a conspicuous place and read it over and over again, embracing the wisdom with all of your being. It will set you free. It will activate the indescribably powerful process of co-creation for your heart's desires. It is the secret to welcoming in the love of your life.

LOVE COACHING PROGRAM

It's ALL About YOU

PERSONAL PLANNER

STEP FOUR: **Embrace It** (New activities)

Exercise 1: Continue your daily Gratitude practice. This time focus on being grateful for your experiences. This includes the good, the great, and the not-so-great types of life experiences. Read each night before going to bed.

Example:

- ♡ I'm grateful for my summer vacation
- ♡ I'm grateful for being asked to join the committee
- ♡ I so appreciate my time at the spa
- ♡ I'm grateful for the lessons I learned from my last love relationship
- ♡ I'm grateful my boyfriend showed me who he really is
- ♡ I so appreciate my job
- ♡ I'm grateful for the feedback; it's helped me grow
- ♡ I'm grateful to be able to exercise
- ♡ I'm grateful for losing that job; I found a new direction

Exercise 2: Think about all of the things you've done to connect with your ideal love match. I know you may be wondering if the list making is ever going to end. Yes, but not before this exercise. You've come a long way. Stay with me – you'll be happy you did. What activities did you participate in that you didn't like or enjoy just in hopes of meeting a potential date? Make a decision to embrace activities you enjoy or want to explore.

Example: golf lessons, bar hopping, ball games, on-line dating, blind dating, etc.

Exercise 3: Forget about dating for a few minutes and make a list of activities you've thought about doing, but haven't. Really get creative and think about what you want to do. It's ok to be nervous about trying new things, but it's definitely not ok to refuse to step outside of your comfort zone. Remember, if you enjoy the activity, then your love connection just might be there enjoying it too!

Examples: photography class, cooking class, golf lessons, joining a corporate board, volunteer activities, etc.

Exercise 4: Continue working on your personal energy zappers list. Reward yourself in some small way for each accomplishment. Keep work and play in balance. You know the old saying, "All work and no play makes Jack a dull boy." Boring is out!

Exercise 5: Surrender and let the *Universal Creative Energy* do the connecting. You're doing your part. Remember: We're talking about surrendering the struggle and angst.

Chapter Thirteen

Part II Conclusion

The steps outlined in this section are based on the experiences of the women in this book; those women who travelled the pathway to welcome in the love of their life. Most of them had challenging journeys. A few walked more quickly into a "substantially compatible" and sustainable love partnership.

All of us would like for our experiences to benefit others, not in the same way they formed and informed us, but in a way that provides insight and assists others in attracting the love relationship of their dreams. I hope you are as inspired by these stories as I was when hearing them. These women have generously shared their life lessons with us, both the victories and the defeats. Use this information to guide your thoughts, intentions, and choices.

Think about their choices and think about the relationship choices you've made. Choices made in ignorance of the possibilities are limited. Choices made from a place of wholeness in heart, body, soul, and mind support you in living your best life and in sharing life with the partner of your dreams. You don't have to settle. You have a choice. You can:

- ✓ Forget about the search
- ✓ Think about the qualities you desire in a life partner
- ✓ Take action to make needed changes
- ✓ Fully embrace your own life

Finding your love connection is possible if you believe it is so and you are willing to make any necessary changes. I hope you've decided to follow my process; ***It's All About You Love Coaching Program***. Even if you're skeptical, I encourage you to try it anyway. You'll be glad you did!

As you read about Jeanne's long journey to her true love, take note of how each of the steps outlined in this section played a role in her successful outcome. She didn't know about the steps, nor did she articulate them in so many words; however, you will become aware of them as I did when hearing her story.

"I married out of fear the first time, out of a sense of duty the second time and finally for love – the right reason, the right man."

Jeanne

Jeanne's Story

Every relationship Jeanne had ended with infidelity or alcoholism. The first college boyfriend was a nice guy; but when Jeanne wasn't around; his motto was, out of sight – out of mind.

She met Hank when she was nineteen. He was twenty-three. Their three year relationship was far from smooth. Jeanne married him for fear of being alone after deciding the "devil" she knew was better than the one she didn't. They had two daughters while he worked two jobs at local bars.

Jeanne spent far too much time alone. Unfortunately, when she asked her husband to leave his second job to spend more time with his family, he chose the job instead and left them.

After Hank's departure Jeanne realized her love of music had also suffered in their marriage. Hank had refused to connect the stereo system in their home. The only music she could listen to was on the car radio. He'd left her guitar packed away somewhere in the basement. She hadn't seen it in seven years.

After their divorce, Jeanne began visiting a local club to sing karaoke. Heartbroken, she found karaoke a great way to let go of her pain. She belted out songs such as, "I Will Survive," and "When Will I Be Loved." Lee, the Karaoke Manager, praised her singing and soon won her heart. She began to enjoy life again, while at the same time ignoring the warning signs of his non-stop drinking. Just when she was about to muster the courage to walk away, she learned she was pregnant with their child. Unsure what to do, she sought counsel from her church minister and tried to find a direction for her life.

Jeanne decided to marry Lee. Lee's father became a source of love and support for her despite his passing three months earlier. Should she tell Lee about his impending fatherhood? This decision was not an easy one. Each time Jeanne felt this angst; she sensed Lee's father's presence and felt an amazing comfort. The message she heard: "Please have this baby to give Lee something to get sober for, something to live for."

Although she knew that plan was likely to fail, she felt it was her duty to marry Lee and take him to a rehabilitation facility. She thought she could fix him with her love and support. His sobriety held for four years until his uncle handed him a brandy at a family wedding. Then Lee fell off the wagon.

Devastated, Jeanne was unable to see herself living through yet another rehabilitation experience with Lee. She made the difficult decision to leave when she found condoms in his jacket pocket – evidence of what she'd suspected all along. "I put myself through hell. I didn't need to," she said. Love had not been a factor. The determination to win at all costs had taken over. The warning signs had flashed brightly. She ignored them again.

Prior to sending him packing, they tried marriage counseling. Jeanne wanted to be a good Christian woman and stand by her man. It was not to be. "The condoms were the key to my jail cell," she told me. After the counselor met with them separately, he told Jeanne privately he could not save Lee; but he could help her with the Al-Anon program.

Knowing she had hit rock bottom, she was ready to stop the relationship rollercoaster ride. Al-Anon saved her life by providing the tools to recognize her repetitive destructive patterns. This program showed her a better way. Faithfully attending meetings three or four times a week, she made a choice never to give anyone else the power to make her feel that bad again. She became clear about what she would and would not accept in her future relationships.

As Jeanne continued healing from her ordeal, she took solace in writing. Messages came through as she opened her heart to being led to a better life. She made the decision to *"just do it"* and followed her dream to move from Idaho to Colorado. She surrounded herself with a network of people to assist in her new career.

With this new beginning, she decided to join an internet dating service and see what might happen. The first year, she had many first dates, but no seconds. Frustrated, she decided not to date but to focus on her new career and family.

When she met cool, good-looking Harry, she was pleased - especially since he treated her so well - a new experience for Jeanne. Although he repeatedly said he did not see a future together, they dated for a year and a half. He ended their relationship the day after Christmas, leaving Jeanne for a woman she knew. Unfortunately, she had fallen in love with Harry.

Although Jeanne walked through life as if someone had sucker-punched her, she somehow found the courage to join an international business association with a strong emphasis on personal empowerment. Through that organization, she became friends with an expert in muscle testing therapy. (Muscle testing is based on the traditional Chinese medicine concept of internal energy channels. It is a non-invasive way to assess energy blockages, organ functioning, food sensitivities, etc., by applying slight pressure to a large muscle under resistance – very interesting stuff).

The muscle testing expert saw her suffering and offered a treatment. After hearing her story, he asked her to say, "Getting rejected by men makes me strong." Jeanne's arm muscles resisted his pressure with a strength she'd never known until that day. That gave her something to think about.

The next meeting of the personal empowerment group was in California, the week her deceased grandmother would have been one hundred years old. Her grandmother's name was Grace; and as they sang, "Amazing Grace," Jeanne melted into tears. She sensed her dear grandmother nearby, providing love and support.

In the next moment, Jeanne's grandfather burst into her consciousness saying over and over how sorry he was for anything he'd done to hurt her. Jeanne said she felt instant forgiveness. She recalled being eight years old when her grandfather told her quite clearly that he loved her, but would never show her love. Wounded deeply by his words, she felt confused when she watched him hug and kiss her cousins. His steadfast refusal to share affection with her created a deep childhood wound.

Jeanne was now in her early forties. Throughout her entire life, she'd only experienced love through rejection. Boyfriends, husbands, ministers, everyone who said they loved her had, in fact, rejected her instead. This foundational programming of a love-pain connection crumbled, and the walls she'd erected around herself came down.

When Jeanne met another man who behaved badly after only six weeks, she immediately walked away. Soon after, she enrolled in a personal empowerment class at her church. At the same time, she reconnected via email with Craig, an old friend who had worked with her father many years ago. Craig's wife was ill, and he'd sent a message that he was concerned about her health.

Initially, the email was lost among the hundreds in Jeanne's email box. By the time she found it, Craig's wife had passed away.

She didn't know what to say. Craig's emails had been to the group of employees that worked together many years ago – Jeanne was one of them. She wanted to respond, but several months passed before she found the words.

Meanwhile, Jeanne was learning about the power of intention, affirmations, and ways to release any remaining blockages to receiving her heart's desire. Embracing the wholeness she now felt in her life, she journaled about her desire for a partner to share her life in every way. The possibility that Craig might be that person never crossed her mind. Craig lived in another state, and she'd known his lovely, sweet wife.

The next time Craig was in town, they made a plan to meet for dinner. As Jeanne was dressing to meet him, the thought occurred to her that he was now single. She hit herself in the head – literally – trying to knock the startling idea out of her mind. When it came again, she berated herself out loud for being such a stupid and desperate woman. When she entered the restaurant and saw him for the first time in many years, she felt a push from behind and a little voice saying, "He's cute, isn't he." No one was there.

Over dinner they enjoyed a wonderful conversation, catching up on old times and each other's lives. As the evening ended, Craig said he was not ready to date again. Yet, when he was ready, he'd like to call. She also thought it best to remain friends, at least for now, still taken aback by her earlier thoughts and experiences.

A few weeks later they began regular communication via phone and email. Craig shared he'd been having long talks with his deceased wife and sensed it would be okay for him to move on with his life. Jeanne and Craig frequently saw each other over the next two months. At Christmas, he flew her to Nebraska to be his date for his company Christmas party. When he asked Jeanne how he should introduce her that evening, she replied, "How about as your fiancé?" The words blurted out, surprising even Jeanne. Craig was also surprised, but thrilled.

Jeanne said, "I waited forty-four years for the love of my life, and he was so worth it. We live, work, love and go to church together. I am so grateful for what we have every day. *Source* answered me in so many ways. It just keeps getting better."

Jeanne's story illustrates the entire process for finding an authentic love connection. When she ended her second marriage, she believed she was finished with men for a long time. Once she realized her need to stop the cycle of attracting broken men, Jeanne was led to a variety of resources that ultimately facilitated and supported growth. Here is a short summary of how this four step process played out for Jeanne:

Step 1: Forget about it – designed to take the focus from searching for a love relationship. This is a critical first step.

In this example Jeanne recognized something was terribly wrong with her love relationships and stopped to re-evaluate. For six months she regularly attended the Al-Anon program and began to focus on what she really wanted in her life. Although not a one-time process for her, in the end she determined to claim her power – to make different choices.

Step 2: Think about it – requires thoughtful consideration of what values and qualities you desire in a romantic partner and in your love relationship or marriage, which ignites the *Law of Attraction.*

When Jeanne took time to think about what she really wanted, the *Universal Creative Energy Source* was enlisted to co-create her life. She deeply desired a new type of romantic relationship, and she also envisioned a more fulfilling career.

Step 3: Just do it – is the action step. Once you've taken time for yourself, created your list, and aligned with the *Universe,* it's time to take action in the direction of your dreams.

Jeanne's decision to "just do it" opened the door for her to take action for change. Going for her dream changed her life in all ways. Thinking about it and just doing it were not linear processes, but stepping stones on Jeanne's ascent to a richer life.

When her last boyfriend started to show his true colors, Jeanne took action right away – something she had never done before. She put a firm stop to the cycle of giving her energy to a lost cause by coming to terms with her childhood traumas.

Step 4: Embrace your life – gives you full responsibility for your choices, your love, your peace, integrity, values, and happiness – all the things vital for a healthy soul-satisfying partnership.

By the time Craig walked into Jeanne's life, she had already embraced a new career and set new intentions. The baggage of the past was placed firmly behind her as Jeanne embraced her new standards and new intentions. The channel was open wide for the *Universe* to co-create with Jeanne her heart's desires.

Forget About It – Think About It – Just Do It – Embrace It

Part III

Fact or Fiction?

Chapter Fourteen

Relationship Myths

Myth, as defined by the Merriam Webster dictionary, is "a false collective belief that is used to justify a social institution." Viewing this definition in the context of a marriage or long-term committed partnership invites us to scrutinize our beliefs about how love relationships work.

Many of us grew up believing the myths we heard about marriage and love relationships. As children we respected our parents, grandparents and other adults, so we accepted what we were told as truth. I never gave much thought to the "wisdom" bestowed on me by the adults in my life until I had my own life changing experience with marriage.

In this chapter, we'll explore common, generally accepted wisdom about love relationships and see how well it reflects real life experiences. As we continue to visit the stories of the women interviewed, you may find yourself questioning your own beliefs. I invite you to consider a more conscious approach to what you believe about love relationships. Some of the happiest couples, like those you've met in this book, no longer subscribe to old-world wisdom.

Keep in mind that most of what we learned about love came from well-intentioned people who loved and raised us with our best interests in mind. However, when their relationship myths are scrutinized in the light of actual experience, the happiest of couples I've met live their lives far from the relationship myths they learned from childhood. They've traded these beliefs for a greater truth that unfolded in their ultimate love relationship.

Myth One

MARRIAGE IS HARD WORK

This particular myth is one of the most popular and most often quoted. Almost everyone I know believes this one to be true - everyone, that is, except for those who have the love of their lives in that singularly palpable way that makes others smile and say, "They are so crazy about each other."

While watching one of my favorite Food Network shows, *The Barefoot Contessa,* Ina Garten (the host of the show) was about to prepare a special dinner for her husband for their 40th wedding anniversary. As she chopped and stirred, she smiled and said that people often asked about the secret to her long and happy marriage. She clearly disagreed with the old saying that marriages are hard work. In fact, she said, "Marriage is not hard work. Actually, it's easy. I want my husband to be happy and he wants me to be happy. It's as simple as that."

The hard work myth has affected many of us for a long, long time. That doesn't mean that marriage never has any drama or trauma. That's simply not possible when two people are intimately involved with one another. Challenges and difficult issues arise in the best of marriages. People get sick or injured, lose their jobs, family members pass away, chaos happens. When things go wrong, great marriages, built on solid ground, have partners that support one another in ways that matter most.

To say that marriage is hard work implies a daily struggle. If a relationship is "hard work" most of the time, it will wear you out. Many of the women interviewed saw their first marriages collapse because of the daily struggle. Their new approach to marriage has them amazed at how much easier their current relationships are in comparison. Their present relationships flow more effortlessly, regardless of the challenges. Both partners remain relaxed and at peace, knowing they can truly trust themselves and each other with their deepest feelings and desires.

It took me by surprise when I heard over and over in the interviews the central feeling of being in an easy flowing relationship that sustained happiness and longevity. Now that I've had that experience myself, it makes sense. The true "wisdom" of a successful relationship comes from finding the love of your life – someone with whom you have an easy flowing connection - almost from the beginning.

As each woman began to tell me her story, the ease and flow was evident from the moment she met the love of her life. No one said her relationship was hard work. No one said her easy, flowing, happy, satisfying relationship came after much hard work. The only hard work I heard mentioned happened in marriages and relationships that eventually failed – in spite of serious efforts to make things work. As we reconsider the "wisdom" of this old adage, think about putting it firmly in the category of "myth."

The following story came from one woman, but is essentially the history of so many of our relationships. Amy had amazing perseverance and thought she too could have a life partner support and love her, if she just worked hard enough.

"The total sacrifice of my life for his became too much. I wanted to be equally yoked with my husband, but I finally realized it was never going to happen with this man."

Amy

Amy's Story

His mother embraced her wholeheartedly, providing the warmth and support she often lacked in her own home. Amy was seventeen and he was eighteen when they met. Like his mother, he was a loving, gentle person. Amy adopted his family, his friends and his lifestyle. Lovingly, she prepared his breakfast, packed his lunch, helped him study for certification exams, and even walked picket lines with him. Those were the wifely duties she'd been taught were essential, so she went about them with all her heart and soul.

After seven years of being a team, they made it official and were married. Their friends and family thought they were a perfect match. Amy continued working, going to college, and completing all of her "wifely duties" until it became overwhelming. Something had to give. Her desire for a career in broadcasting received no support from her husband, so she made the difficult decision to leave school.

That total sacrifice of her life for his became too much, and she wanted to explore some of her own interests. She became a professional hula dancer – with no support from her husband. She worked for a modeling agency – with no support from her husband. She tried real estate – again with no support from her husband. Not only was he unsupportive of her activities, but also he refused to attend church with her. Instead, he partied with his friends, often drinking heavily.

Amy had outgrown the partying phase of her life and wanted to move on. She wanted to establish a solid adult lifestyle and share mutual interests. His only interest appeared to be his own life, which now included excessive drinking and partying.

On their first anniversary, Amy cried tears of despair at what her life had become. She moved out of their home to give him time to think and hopefully mature. Amy asked him to join her in couples counseling, but he wasn't interested.

Six months passed. One day while she was shopping, she saw him with another woman. This was difficult, even though she knew their relationship had been finished for some time. She had matured and knew that her heart's desire was for a man with whom she could be "equally yoked." That wasn't going to happen with her husband – now or ever – so she made the hardest decision of her life. She ended her marriage.

For most of the next year, Amy had upsetting dreams. Her guilt and misery were calmed by listening to music, journaling, and talking herself through all the pain. She slowly walked out of despair and into her own life – one day at a time. Each step became easier and easier as she let it all go. Before she'd really figured out who she was and what made her happy, she was introduced to a new man. Amy jumped headlong into a relationship with him. They argued frequently and parted after six years of turmoil.

Amy prayed for help to find a new place to live and a new job. When her prayers were answered, once again she felt the freedom to re-create her life. This time she decided to make different choices – hopefully better ones.

At thirty-years-old, with no career, partial college credits, and no clear intention for her own life, she realized that she'd been trying to do the impossible – fix broken men. She spent the next six months alone, discovering what brought her joy and peace.

When she started dating again, she quickly learned she didn't know the rules of engagement. Like so many other women, she didn't understand why there were no second dates after having such fun the first time out. Amy's male friends let her in on the secret that most men know and women often don't. Just because you had a nice time, good conversation and an overall fun experience doesn't mean there was a love connection.

Amy's advice for women is to take responsibility for your choices and stop assuming that every guy who takes you out and says he had a good time is your future soul mate. She set her own boundaries and became much smarter about how to handle the men in her life. She says men like fast cars and faster relationships. Know that going in, and be prepared to own the choices you make.

Smiling wryly, she told me she'd been on the "catch and release" program, but she was always the one being thrown back into the pond. When she realized what had been happening, she was able to recognize the sports fishermen for who they were. With that understanding, she could play in that pond at will, knowing the consequences.

What she really wanted was to be joined with a loving, supportive partner in every way. She was over being a plaything to be tossed aside at the whim of someone else. She became more discerning in her choices. While still learning the rules of engagement, Amy began blogging about her dating experiences. One evening, she received a response and was impressed with the writer's eloquence. His name was Jonathan. They became cyberspace friends. Amy wasn't ready yet for a committed relationship because she knew her self-awareness was still a work in progress. Family and friends often asked why she was still single at thirty. Not only were their questions annoying, but also they sometimes sent her into a pity-party. She wondered, "What's wrong with me?" She knew the answer was "nothing." Nothing was wrong with her.

The men she'd met thus far were not right and she knew that. Unpleasant experiences with the wrong men were far too numerous and exhausting, so Amy made the conscious determination that the right partner would be available when the time was right.

Emails with Jonathan became phone calls. After a few months, they decided to meet. He made a three hour drive to join Amy and her friends for a STYX concert. LA traffic was horrible. When he called to let her know he'd be late, she offered to order his dinner and have it kept warm. After they met he let her know how impressed he was by her thoughtful gesture. She thought he was adorable, very cute – but short. She was taller than Jonathan, and she also loved wearing heels.

They had a great time at the concert, but she knew the relationship was impossible. He was moving out of state to be closer to his two children, and she wanted no part of a long distance relationship. The blogging continued about her dating experiences and Jonathon added a "very cool" blog entry about their night out. Their phone calls became more random, and they soon lost touch as their busy lives got in the way.

A few months later, Amy opened her MySpace page and Jonathan was gone. When he deleted her from his friends list, he disappeared from her web page. When she called to ask what happened, Jonathan told her he had been seeing someone who demanded that he delete female friends from his profile. He admitted regretting that action immediately after doing it. As they talked, Amy counseled him on following his instincts.

They agreed that he would come for a visit so they could talk further in person. They met over dinner and the conversation flowed; two friends talking – nothing more. After meeting her friends and dancing for several hours, they went back to her place and continued talking. After talking for hours, he turned her face to his and kissed her sweetly – something he wished he'd done the first time they met. She pulled him close and kissed him passionately. It felt right - completely comfortable.

Neither of them could stop thinking about each other. She thought about all of the reasons it wouldn't work, but she couldn't wait to see him and talk to him again. He drove three hours each way to see her, knowing soon he'd be even further away when he moved out of state.

Jonathan invited her to his retirement party where she met his friends and family. As they departed, he gave her a card; and for the first time, he said, "I love you." She was overcome with emotion – unable to speak. "I know you can't say it, but I know you feel it", he said as they hugged goodbye.

As Amy watched him drive away, tears poured down her face. She didn't stop crying for most of the week. Even though she'd asked *God* to bring her love when the time was right, she simply couldn't accept it now that it was here. Her trust had been abused too many times.

Jonathan returned a week later and made it clear he wanted her in his life. They dated for a few months. After accepting a beautiful engagement ring, she took a leap of faith, quit her job, left her previous life, and moved to be with him.

On her wedding day, there was not one thought or question about whether she was doing the right thing. She had no regrets. Her life now was one hundred and eighty degrees different from the one she left in Los Angeles - the life that included socializing with Hollywood stars, travelling to exotic places like Hong Kong and Italy, shopping and working out. "I love this man and I'd marry him all over again," she told me with tears of joy beautifully streaming down her face.

Myth Two

OPPOSITES ATTRACT

This particular myth is somewhat true in the sense that people are often attracted to others who have opposite characteristics or completely different lifestyles. Starting a relationship with someone who's your opposite can be fun and exciting. It's a way to experience things you might never do on your own. I don't deny the initial attraction part of this "wisdom."

However, the implication that "opposites" are good choices for long-term relationships is another story. What you thought was interesting, cute, or endearing in the beginning of a relationship may become seriously annoying and exasperating when routinely experienced.

When your partner wants to spend every vacation and most available weekends camping and hiking and you'd like to go to "Camp Marriott" or somewhere else, the stage is set for frustrating confrontations. The balance of give and take and the enjoyment of shared mutual interests soon disappear. As a result, separate lives begin to develop as the couple spends more and more time apart. The alternative is that someone always gives in, sacrificing his/her own desires for what the partner wants. Over time, this leads to feeling unheard and unfulfilled.

Think about what it might mean to the quality of your relationship to be with your total opposite. Marrying your identical twin isn't the answer either. Balance is really what most of us want in our relationships. Differences can be complimentary when there's balance. Men and women intrinsically have differences in many areas of their lives. When those differences are understood, honored, met with respect and a willingness to listen and share, the result is harmony.

Harmony and compatibility in a love relationship fosters growth and indescribable joy. Contentment ensues for both people. It's fun and rewarding to share common interests. It's also important to support each other in individual activities.

Like many women, I love spending part of my leisure time shopping. I once had the romantic notion of shopping with my husband, holding hands, perusing the shops for hours, stopping for tea or ice cream, and generally being in couples shopping heaven. I've learned this is not going to be how it is most of the time.

I shop alone for personal items and thoroughly enjoy myself for hours, knowing my sweet wonderful husband is happier engaged in his own pursuits. My couples shopping fantasy is only in play a few times during the year when we are together for holiday or special occasion shopping. I accept that most men do not like shopping, period. Home improvement stores may be an exception. Check out the faces of men you see shopping with their partner. Many of them sit outside the stores waiting. This difference is one my husband and I completely understand and sometimes even joke about.

What you like to do in your spare time, what you like to spend money on, and how you prefer to live your life are too important to hold onto the relationship myth, "opposites attract." Establishing a high level of compatibility with your partner can be a real struggle when there are opposing spiritual, physical, emotional, and intellectual preferences and values.

When there is a constant battle of wills, or one person acquiesces more often than the other, the balance shifts. It doesn't take long for the relationship dynamic to shift far enough for us to feel it. You will instinctively know when you have sufficient balance between your differences and similarities, and that's important for long-term compatibility.

Some of us try to rationalize our feelings away, but the reality remains unchanged. There may not be sufficient compatibility with some people to sustain a long-term healthy and happy partnership. It may be a case of trying to jam a round peg into a smaller square hole. It may seem to fit, but the void around the edges remains.

Trust your "intuition." Tune in to your true feelings. The powerful physical attraction you may initially share will not be enough to sustain the relationship through the many trials of life if the intellectual, spiritual, and emotional attraction is lacking. Do you really want the daily challenge of trying to create harmony where little exists?

There are many stories in this book of women who tried with much heart and bravery to accommodate a partner who did not share their goals, beliefs, aspirations, and/or lifestyle. Their relationships eventually failed because they didn't share enough compatibility upon which to build a foundation of true partnership.

Most likely, you won't need to make a list to convince yourself of the merits of the relationship. You'll feel the balance or imbalance, regardless of how hard you try to overlook the basic lack of compatibility. Trust yourself. As you read the next story, think about what compatibility means for the future happiness and longevity of your love relationship. If what you share in common is consistently eclipsed by your differences, you may want to reconsider the possibility for happy longevity.

"Now that I know what's out there, I'm in heaven. I won't settle anymore."

Heather

Heather's Story

The rough and tumble environment of the oil business was not what Heather expected when she married her husband at age twenty-one. He was frequently away on the oil rig, and she tried to make the best of it despite their differences. The birth of their child added to the challenges. In the end, she found it impossible to reconcile their present lifestyle with her needs for a more settled life for herself and her daughter. When the marriage ended, she moved to a more supportive and familiar environment.

Six years later, Heather met and married the man who was everything she'd been missing. He was her best friend with a solid career and map for their future. Because he was a planner, initially, she felt comfortable knowing the next step on the roadmap for their future. As time passed, their opposite personalities became more evident.

Her intent had been to connect with someone who could provide what she'd been missing in her first marriage. That decision would be a long and disheartening life lesson for Heather. By nature, she was an adventurer. Athletic and active, she loved being surprised and spontaneous more often than her husband found comfortable. Her busy life as a broker and raising children kept her distracted for many years.

Heather was not unhappy, but she wasn't truly happy and satisfied either. Sex had fallen off the radar screen years ago, and she missed that part of her life. Recalling a visit to Hawaii, she realized how much she missed being by the water.

The ocean held a special place for Heather, one she could not stop thinking about. The life she was trying to live sat squarely on her chest like an eight hundred pound gorilla. She knew there had to be a drastic change for her own well-being and survival. The decision to actually live life instead of enduring it came as a shock to family and friends.

When Heather announced she was leaving her home and career and moving to Hawaii, her loved ones thought she'd gone crazy, especially in light of the circumstances. She had no specific plan for work or living arrangements.

Her passion for living life authentically and modeling that value for her daughter became too compelling to ignore. Though void of a detailed plan, she had a belief in her ability to find the new life she craved. With enough money to provide a new beginning, Heather left her home and settled into a rented space on the beautiful island of Maui. There, she felt at peace among the small community of surfers and outdoor enthusiasts living near the ocean.

When it came time to search for a job, Heather thought, "What am I going to do? There are no broker jobs here." When she thought about the things she knew how to do, the previous jobs she'd had, she said, "I've done upholstery – that's what I will do." She bought a sewing machine and started going door to door looking for work. One step at a time, she built a business to support herself and her daughter. The life she created was exactly what she intended. She believed that not only was her dream life a real possibility, but also it was attainable.

As she worked on building her business, a friend mentioned several times that she should meet Lynn Matthews Davis, a local shop owner who might possibly provide more business opportunities. Heather didn't give it too much thought, although she assumed she'd meet Lynn someday.

A busy woman with plenty on her plate, she ran along the ocean every morning to stay in shape. She often noticed another woman running as well. They'd smile and nod and keep to their own path. One day, the lady stopped Heather and asked if she was a tourist or a local. Her name was Lynn Matthews Davis.

They quickly became friends. Soon, Lynn and her family took Heather and her daughter in, which opened their world in the small island community. After that, opportunities were abundant. Heather was asked to coach the girls in the school's first track and field program. She'd never coached anyone before, but she was a mom and a very good runner. What more could she need?

Still living in the ocean-front rental space, she walked outside one day to find a strange man in the front yard with his surfing gear. He looked up and their eyes locked. Her landlord introduced him as a friend and house guest. The rapport was immediate. They had fun talking, eating, and surfing, but Heather was uncomfortable. She did not want anything to detract from her focus on building this new life. Her bigger plans didn't include living forever in a rental situation or a romantic relationship.

Zack, the house guest with the magnetic eyes, went back to the mainland but occasionally called. In the meantime Heather and her daughter moved into their own condominium. When she decided to fly to the mainland to run a marathon with a girlfriend, she called Zack to let him know. He suggested they all meet for dinner. They had a wonderful time, but Heather, sensing the strong attraction, remained somewhat uncomfortable.

Zack flew to Maui frequently for his business and often spent time with Heather and her daughter. While there, he became her daughter's surfing coach. He was always patient and kind in his efforts to assist her daughter in this challenging sport. Heather was feeling a keen interest in this man, but she was unsure of how to respond.

One night after dinner, he suggested going for a drink. Heather agreed. On the drive back, Zack said he wanted to show her a pretty spot to watch the sunset. When they got out of the car to look at the stunning ocean view, he pulled her close for a kiss. Heather lost all sense of time and space. The kiss was amazing. The experience was unlike anything she'd ever felt before. This kiss had thrown her "completely off base."

Reeling from that experience, she was caught in a web of conflicting needs and desires. It was clear the schools on the island were not challenging her daughter. Heartbroken and in a torrent of tears, they left, returning to their former life. Heather decided to try one more time to work things out with her husband, but she couldn't stop crying when she tried to fall asleep in his arms. There would be no working it out.

Five years later, after her daughter's high school graduation, Heather moved back to Maui where she felt her heart belonged. She bought a house, started a new business, and was once again loving life. Occasionally, she thought about Zack, but surprisingly, given the small size of the island community, she never saw him.

She'd been on the island for over a year when it happened. One day after taking photographs by the ocean, she started toward her car to leave. A strong feeling that she needed one more picture interrupted her exit. As she headed back to the beach, a cyclist whizzed by. Even though she only saw his back, she knew it was

Zack. She called out to him, but he couldn't hear her. Heather ran back to her car, drove ahead of him and pulled to the side of the road. When he stopped, the sight of her nearly took his breath away. He'd moved there as well and had been in a relationship for several years. Genuinely happy for each other, they agreed to keep in touch as friends.

Later the same day, she saw him again at the garden shop, then again at the grocery store that afternoon. He called her that night while she was having dinner with a friend. He was sitting outside looking at the stars, unable to get her out of his mind. They talked about remaining friends, but both knew that would not be possible. The attraction was undeniable.

Though the road forward was unclear, they knew what they had together was unlike anything they'd ever experienced. The intimacy they shared on every level couldn't be broken by time or distance. Heather was no longer willing to settle for anything less. Zack and Heather are now happily married.

Experience taught her the true value of compatibility, and the connection she experienced with Zack was undeniable. Heather smiles beautifully and says she has no regrets. Having known true love is far better than never having known it, regardless of the final outcome. In sharing her story, Heather hopes to inspire single women to follow their dreams.

Her advice: "Don't give in or settle for less than your heart's desire."

Myth Three

TRUE LOVE COMES ALONG ONLY ONCE IN A LIFETIME

This myth is an incredibly popular one, deeply embedded in mind, body and soul for many of us. It is the stuff movies are made of. We hear it from early childhood, reinforced through fairy tales and bedtime stories. Snow White, Cinderella, and dozens of other classics are just a few examples. Hundreds of romantic movies imprint this belief with vigor. We want lives like those portrayed on the silver screen.

There are two problems with the belief that there's only one perfect partner for each of us. The first problem comes when the strength of that belief causes someone to search relentlessly for the tiniest flaw in every potential relationship. The resulting angst can overwhelm otherwise good instincts.

Looking for the perfect person overshadows the real desire to have our perfect partner. That doesn't mean we have to settle. However, we do need to know what characteristics and values are truly important for our own well-being and happiness. I've encountered countless family members and friends who often shake their heads and sigh about their loved one's desperate search for the perfect person. They witness the struggle, see the heartbreaks, and try to offer advice and assistance, but most often they feel helpless.

The stress of searching and eliminating partners in the context of wanting to find the one and only perfect mate is a powerful force for blocking the very thing you want. People who've found the love of their lives unwittingly contribute to the tragedy of this belief. Once you have "it," you cannot imagine being with anyone else. That's understandable.

If you are truly happy and satisfied with your love relationship, you aren't going to be looking for another one. When you have the relationship of your dreams, the gratitude you feel for it far outweighs any second guessing. Gratitude, joy, and deep satisfaction confirm that this is the only person in the world for us. He or she is "the one" – in that place and time.

However, life dramatically changes with the permanent departure of one of the partners. There are many ways for a life partner to leave us. This is the second problem with this myth.

Consider all the circumstances that could suddenly leave a person without his/her true love. Are people doomed to a life absent from the most intimate of relationships? Must they settle for something less, something nice, but not amazing - something workable, but not soul-satisfying?

One of your first thoughts might be, "If there's more than one perfect partner, how do I pick the right one?" I encourage you to shift away from this way of thinking about your true love as a one-time only experience. Instead, consider the possibility that the *Universe* is co-creating your heart's desire, regardless of your current circumstance.

While reading the next story, decide for yourself what you believe.

"My life changed when I decided to stop settling for bad treatment, for something less than I deserved."

Audrey

Audrey's Story

When Audrey and her boyfriend of four years, Todd, graduated from college, he accepted an assignment as a journalist to cover the Olympics in Korea. Their plan was to become engaged and plan their wedding when he returned from Korea. However, that plan abruptly unraveled. Their parents knew each other; and soon, Todd's parents broke some unexpected news to Audrey's parents. Now Audrey's parents were left to tell their daughter the harsh news. After only a few months away, Todd had eloped with another woman.

Audrey was shocked and dismayed. Todd had given her no warning, no phone call, not even an email or letter. She'd thought they were in love. It took a while to recover from this sudden dismissal from his life. When she felt better, she decided a change of venue was in order and moved to California.

She found it exhilarating to be single and free to explore a social life as an adult. It was fun meeting new people in a totally new environment. Two years later, she'd had enough and decided to return to her home state. There she reconnected with old girlfriends, one of whom had recently been unceremoniously "dumped" by her boyfriend. One night they decided to go out to commiserate. As they ordered drinks, they noticed two good looking guys nearby. The men noticed them as well, and those initial conversations turned into love relationships.

Eventually they each married the man they'd met that night. The trust that had been broken in Audrey's earlier relationship was solid from the beginning with this new man. She described the relationship with her husband, Leon, as "Easy. No wondering if I could trust him – no games." He was without question her best friend, the one responsible for dissolving her past insecurities about men. The twenty pounds she'd put on since the surprising break-up with Todd melted away as well.

Knowing she was loved unconditionally created space for Audrey to relax and fully enjoy life. They were inseparable from the beginning, marrying two years later. Leon was the love of her life. After purchasing a home, they settled into married life, doing almost everything together. Audrey was living the life she'd always wanted.

Leon and Audrey had entrepreneurial spirits and together planned to begin a new business venture. They often joked about winning the million dollars needed to start their business. Life was good and fun and beautiful.

Four blissful years later, Leon received a special birthday gift from her parents – a private flying adventure in an open cockpit airplane – something he'd always dreamed about. Uncharacteristically, Audrey stayed home that day to participate in a community yard sale. For several hours, everything went as planned. Then the unimaginable happened. The plane crashed, instantly killing both Leon and the pilot. Audrey was utterly and completely devastated. Tragically, she lost the love of her life and became a widow at the age of thirty.

Audrey had always been upbeat and positive about life, but after Leon's death, she was lost. Unable to deal with the daily reminders and the best intentions of friends and family, she moved to a condominium in the mountains to recover and find some sense of herself again.

The pain intensified when a check arrived from the insurance company for one million dollars. She no longer wanted the money. All she wanted was Leon. She not only was the widow everyone whispered about, but also she was a rich widow, benefitting from her husband's cruel death. The pain was unbearable.

After mourning her loss for over a year working through the pain, she found herself craving normalcy and companionship. When her friends and family encouraged her to move on with her life, she did – or tried to do so. One day, while living alone in the small mountain town, she saw a familiar face – one of the boys she'd known in high school. They met over coffee and soon renewed their friendship. A few months later, Audrey and Lance became more than friends.

Lance confided he'd been recently released from a drug rehabilitation program. Thinking he was cured, Audrey continued their relationship, all the while resisting his urges for them to be married. Discovering she was pregnant changed her mind. On the third day of their honeymoon in Hawaii, Lance disappeared for several days. The lure of drugs had been too much for him to handle now that he could once again afford them. This began a long and expensive battle for her freedom and the baby's safety.

For over a decade, Audrey tried to find someone with whom to share her life. Her efforts were in vain. She secretly believed that she'd already had the love of her life and didn't deserve another, especially since many of her friends had never found their true love.

Audrey thought someday she'd find someone to marry and have a family, but she believed she'd have to settle for something less than the wonderful connection she had with Leon. She was sure no one could match what she'd experienced with her first husband.

The results of her belief system, subconsciously and consciously, created the perfect environment for attracting the wrong men. She dated men who drank too much, men who were controlling, men who weren't trustworthy, men who made her feel like she was the one with the problem. Many played games – pretending to be available when they weren't, lavishing and withholding affection at will, or acting charming, like they were everyone's best friend.

All of those behaviors were the red flags Audrey needed to end the cycle of craziness. After several bad relationships, and in the wake of her loss, Audrey had had enough. Her plan to settle for a man she wouldn't love as much as Leon (so it wouldn't hurt so much if she lost him) went out the window.

Fortunately Audrey's story has a happy ending, but not until she made a pivotal decision. She gave herself permission to be loved again by a man who would treat her well and love her unconditionally. When she relaxed into that decision, she felt more peace and happiness than she'd allowed herself to feel since her beloved's death.

Her steady circle of supportive girlfriends had planned their annual weekend in Vail, Colorado. Audrey was ready and looked forward to having a good time. She gave in to what life had to offer, but no more settling. That weekend, a girlfriend introduced her to one of her male friends – a nice, good looking man. Audrey's girlfriends all thought he'd be a perfect distraction.

He turned out to be more than a distraction. The moment she met Jackson and saw his smile, there was a connection. She was tempted to think he was just a handsome, charming player like the others; but within several months, Audrey knew she would give this relationship a chance. By their third date, she felt the love connection in her heart. How did she know? She felt the trust, the joy, and the complete happiness she'd longed for, but had thought might never happen again.

He wasn't perfect, but he was perfect for her. They've been married for eighteen months and are excitedly awaiting the arrival of their first child. Audrey is forty-two years old. What she did that day when she jettisoned her plan to settle for something less than true love was connect with the *Universal Creative Energy* to co-create her new reality. Audrey's story is proof that you can find another true love. Her message to any doubters, "Get a copy of the movie, *The Secret* and watch it over and over and over."

Myth Four

ALL YOU NEED IS LOVE

We've all heard the fabulous Beatles song, *All You Need is Love.* It's a sentiment we want to believe, maybe even cling to out of our need to be loved absent any other requirements. Everyday life has so many lists of to-do's, complications, and demands of us. This song lyric sounds simple enough, inviting, maybe even mesmerizing. We really want to believe these beautiful words, even though most of us probably have at least a tickle of doubt about them. So here's the good news – they're true. The not so great news is – they're also not the truth.

You may be thinking, how is this possible? How can something be true and untrue at the same time? The answer lies in the context. Love alone will not feed you, pay the bills, or take care of your basic needs to live in this world. Nor will feeling romantic love for someone sustain a long-term relationship or marriage. Love must inspire action in the direction of respecting and supporting the loved person, object, animal, cause or community. Talking about how much we love something or someone only goes so far. Love is more than a lovely sentiment or romantic feeling.

Of course, I believe love is the root of all good things. *Spirit* is love; we were created out of love and are here to be loving people. Therefore, to say "All I need is love" is a universal truth in the context of love giving birth to action. True love is easily demonstrated by matched partners when they take their foundational value of love and build a sustainable loving, mutually respectful relationship through supportive actions. The words themselves can only be true when they are given life. The sweetest renditions of this sentiment die quickly in the presence of opposing behaviors. Actions do speak louder than words.

What does this really mean for someone looking for his/her love match? I encourage singles to think through what love means in the context of a relationship. Think about your previous love relationships or marriage(s). Did you both take time to lift up your relationship through loving, supportive actions, or did your love die from neglect or abuse? What behaviors did you accept just because he said "I love you?" What did you overlook that was really a red flag trying to get your attention? Love isn't really authentic love if it isn't supported by loving action.

So if those special words, "I love you" accompanied by genuine intense romantic feeling aren't enough, what else do we need? We need *right action*. This may sound like a strange concept to you right now, but I hope you'll let the idea sit with you for a while as you read more. By *right action* I mean behaviors that support a solid relationship between two committed partners. Wanting something isn't a magic formula for acquisition.

There are many things love alone cannot sustain. Bad behaviors will eat away at the very foundation of a love relationship. You read the chapter on *Trust*. In the beginning of a love relationship, dating is the means by which two people get to know each other and build trust over time or not. Now here's the critical juncture in the road; whether each person has developed his/her ability to see relationship red flags. Yes, red flags - those signs and signals our gut nudges us to heed. Yet, we deny them in the name of love, relationship, or coupledom.

I was really good at living in denial about everything that ultimately culminated in the demise of my first marriage. *All you need is love* resonated with me so completely I was able to keep on believing we would be fine. However, we weren't fine – at least I was far from fine after twenty plus years of denying, overlooking, placating, forgetting and giving without receiving. I craved reciprocity. It wasn't there; and no matter how hard I tried, it never came. I decided martyrdom wasn't for me. I needed a balanced partnership – something I was pretty sure didn't exist. Now I know it does exist if both people know how to be in loving relationship.

What I know now that I didn't know in my first marriage is that two people in love need to grow together through mutual intention. Mutual intention means both people are awake and happily participating in building a life together that meets each individual's needs. Building a deeply satisfying life with another requires each person to contribute ideas, thoughts, feelings, work - anything needed to promote growing together rather than apart. It's far easier to make assumptions than to develop productive communication skills and actually put them in play.

Of course, there will be bumps along the way. Life gets busy and everyone can get off track from time to time. The critical difference between unhappy couples and couples who are thriving is their ability to recognize what's happening and engage in course correction before the relationship or marriage is permanently derailed. This is a vital love connection skill well worth the effort to learn and practice.

Anyone who's been through a relationship or marriage dissolution hopefully learned volumes about what did not work. In the painful aftermath it's easy to forget about what was productive and did keep the relationship going for as long as it did. I encourage you to take time to reflect on how you handled conflict in the past and what things you did that contributed to harmony. In other words, what were your positive contributions and what skills did you lack that possibly created unnecessary pain? Doing this short exercise should help to accelerate your ability to be part of a successful, happy couple.

And by the way, I'm assuming something as I write this chapter. My assumption is that there is authentic love as the foundation of a relationship or marriage. I decided to include this caveat after I recalled several stories of two people marrying with eyes wide open about their mutual regard for one another absent being in love. Staying in a love relationship or marrying someone you're not in love with defies my understanding. All I can say is, don't do it. Don't do it if you ever want to feel deeply and completely loved, adored and cherished.

With that out of the way, I'm going to share my recipe for creating a sustainable loving and mutually satisfying love relationship and marriage. Building on authentic love, two people need to know how to talk with each other in agreement and in disagreement. You may have learned at least two very unhelpful ways of handling conflict by watching family and friends. You're not alone if you have practiced either one of these techniques: saying nothing or yelling. Neither will result in the growth of your relationship. You instinctively know this from experience.

To your foundation of love add: the skills to talk with your partner calmly and respectfully. Learn how to hold your tongue when you're too angry or upset to rationally talk about the issue. No one is really listening when he/she is being yelled at by the partner. Yes, you love your partner, but you're really pissed off in the moment. May I suggest a recess, a walk in the fresh air, a cup of tea, a hot bath, anything that will keep your mouth from spewing forth words you'll most likely later regret. Put away your inner child that has to be right or demands to be heard right now. Speaking harshly or shouting at the one you love chips away at what you're building together.

To that add: doing things together. Thriving couples know it's important to share household responsibilities and discuss any feelings of imbalance. And there's more. Happy couples engage in shared activities: playing board or card games, hiking, travelling, volunteering, hobbies, movies, cooking, reading and anything else they may find interesting. On the opposite end of the spectrum are couples who've lost their way in fostering emotional and intellectual intimacy. They spend very little time together. In fact, when they are in the same room, communication is often minimal, restricted to mundane daily details or senseless arguing.

Thriving couples regularly communicate well, know how to handle conflict, share mutual interests, and support one another's goals and individual interests. One person can have an interest not shared by his/her partner and that is actually a good thing, unless of course this activity dominates all leisure time. So often women in particular relinquish their friends and activities they love only to feel resentment. In healthy relationships there is time for individual interests within reasonable time parameters – each couple decides.

Hopefully this chapter has given you a basis with which to determine what works best for you and your partner. Only you can decide what your needs are within the context of your love partnership. The most important message here is for you to take time to think about what actions or behaviors support a thriving love connection and what you've learned from the past you don't want to repeat. There is no substitute for learning to talk effectively with one another. And yes, that includes physical intimacy. Great sex will not compensate for poor levels of emotional or intellectual intimacy in the long-term.

As you read this next story about Ann, think about your own relationship history. Have you ever settled for less than you should have from a love relationship partner or spouse? Ann learned a valuable lesson - love in action is required to support and sustain a marriage. The words, "I Love You" can be hollow and almost meaningless, if they stand alone. I hope you enjoy reading about Ann's journey and discover any messages you might need to hear.

"When someone shows you who he is, accept it. He will never change."

Ann

Ann's Story

What a jerk - he was laughing at everything and driving like an idiot. Ann was relieved he was her friend's date instead of hers. Instantaneously, she decided she didn't like him. What a conundrum – so handsome and funny, yet so brash and irresponsible.

One year later they met again, and this time the chemistry between them was undeniable. He still drove like a wild man and never took anything too seriously, but when she was with him she could relax and enjoy herself. The connection she felt with his family was also comforting. They immediately loved her and the sentiment was mutual. Their easy-going family dynamic was a totally different world from the one Ann had known.

Quite the serious perceptive child, Ann attempted to cook meals for her family at age eight. Dad wasn't happy when he came home after work if the house wasn't tidy and dinner wasn't cooking. Ann was housekeeper, chef, and keeper of the peace whenever possible. Meeting irresponsible Russell in college was just what she needed - a welcome distraction.

They married after dating for three years. Ann assumed they'd have a normal happy life together. From the outside everything looked perfectly American middle class with this family – two children and a house with two working parents. But things began to change very early in this seventeen year marriage. Ann worked full time as a school teacher, tutored children in her spare time, and did all of the cooking, cleaning, yard work, homework assistance and after school activities. Russell could not keep a job and was frequently either unemployed or under-employed. Even then he did not share in the home care or parenting responsibilities.

In retrospect, Ann recalls never having time to do anything just for herself. She couldn't remember ever reading a book or going to a movie – just endless work. One day her adult son remarked that he'd never seen her just sit down to relax or read. If she was sitting she was folding laundry or grading papers – never just resting. The lessons from her childhood had been imprinted well. She'd be the responsible one - no matter the cost.

One day she overheard Russell talking to the neighbor. He said he actually liked being laid off. Ann was so good at taking care of the family, she really liked her job and that was fine by him. Shortly thereafter panic attacks intruded in her life. As a result, she knew she couldn't keep up with all of her responsibilities. What she didn't know at the time was things were about to get even worse.

Russell started coming home later than usual. He worked at a restaurant, so this was something she could easily overlook. She also overlooked the two notes she found in his car from two different women – he was great at explaining away any clues he was misbehaving. Then one night the assistant manager of the restaurant called near midnight asking for Russell. He'd told Ann he wouldn't be home until 1:00 AM. Once again he came up with a somewhat plausible explanation.

Divorce had never been considered an option in Ann's family. Years earlier her sister had divorced and subsequently incurred intense disapproval from her entire family. Then the unthinkable happened. Her parents announced they were splitting. One week later Ann made her own announcement – she was finished with her marriage as well. The panic attacks stopped, and she felt happy and healthy for the first time in years. She saw Russell only once in the next six years, and that was from a distance at one of their son's school events.

But this relationship would not end. Russell had moved out of state after their divorce, finding it too painful to remain in close proximity to Ann. Being friends wasn't working for him. Then one day as Ann exited the car to meet her son for lunch, Russell appeared. Father and son had been together that morning, so out of politeness Ann invited Russell to join them. She was shocked when he accepted. Following a mildly pleasant lunch, they reconnected over regular telephone conversations. Dating followed, and Russell eventually relocated again to be nearer Ann.

One day their daughter asked if they'd ever consider remarrying. Russell responded that it would be up to her mother, but he was definitely interested. Ten months after reconnecting, they decided to remarry. Ann said Russell cried throughout the ceremony with the justice of the peace. When I asked her how she felt that day, she reported two reactions. First, it felt so right to have her family back together again – their children and his parents as well. She'd really missed his family when they were divorced. Her second reaction was the feeling that he must really love her deeply, given his tears during their wedding ceremony. Afterwards he'd held her tightly and sobbed for what seemed like a very long time.

You may be thinking this story will have a happy ending just like the others you've read so far. And there is a happy ending, just not the one you're expecting. Read on and you will see what I mean and hopefully take away valuable lessons along the way.

Ann and Russell soon began to grow apart once again. Over the course of the next twenty years Ann became increasingly devoted to her spiritual development, while Russell marched steadily down a very different path. He seemed content to watch television and concentrate on his sports interests while practicing the fine art of doing nothing. He was a master at letting Ann do it all. She'd grown accustomed to the status quo with Russell, but this time her discontent was simmering just beneath the surface.

His approach to life as a victim was alien to everything she believed. The love and respect she once felt for him was eroding in spite of her desire to see it through. She wondered how she could possibly divorce him a second time. She couldn't come to terms with doing this to another human being – not a second time. She would seek counsel from her close friends – those dear women she'd become so close to on her spiritual journey. What she wanted most was clarity.

We're all familiar with the old saying, "Be careful what you ask for because you just might get it." One Tuesday night Ann shared her request for clarity with her circle of friends. These were powerful women, connected to *Spirit* and ready to support their friend during this challenging time. Wednesday morning a phone call came for Russell. The woman caller declined to leave a message. Ann was busy and did not think any more about it. The next day the same woman called again and this time left a phone number. On Saturday the phone rang again and Russell answered it this time. Ann thought he was talking to a salesperson, given the coldness of his tone. She heard him say he wasn't interested and then he hung up.

When she asked him who he was talking to, all the color drained from his face. She pressed him to tell her what was wrong. He said you are going to be very mad at me. When we were married the first time, I had an affair with a woman and she got pregnant. That was my daughter's sister – she wants to meet me. "And you said you weren't interested?" Ann was stunned by his response. She told me in that very moment she decided to take the high road. Their daughter had died at the age of thirty from cancer. This potentially new daughter would be welcomed into their family, and together Ann and Russell would get to know and support her.

This magnanimous plan was not supported by Russell. After Ann's insistence, Russell called the woman back and asked for his daughter's phone number. He called and let her know he'd thought about it, changed his mind, and did want to meet her. Ann wanted to go along, but Russell would have none of that. Several hours later he returned and told Ann he'd met his daughter, her husband and child. He was pleased with the visit, but he did not agree to Ann's plans to invite them for a weekend barbeque. Russell and his newly discovered daughter talked periodically on the telephone for several months, but that was the extent of their relationship.

This was not sitting well with Ann. One night she could not sleep, so she went downstairs to sit in the living room. She sat all night thinking about her life with Russell. Everything that had happened between them ran through her mind like a movie in fast forward. The more she saw, the madder she became. She'd forgiven many things over the years, but this was too much. He'd never come through for her, never supported their children. Now he was abandoning this child all over again. He'd never been financially responsible and lied to her constantly. He hadn't even been going to work most of the time even when he had a job.

Ann was crying when Russell came downstairs the next morning. She let him have it – all of her frustration, anger and disappointment. She made it clear that his willingness to let her carry the entire load was no longer palatable. She could not overlook the abandonment of this new daughter on top of a laundry list of other failures to be a real man, husband, and father to their children. Disappointment was the word she used to describe their relationship. The love and respect she once had for him had finally evaporated. This was her get out of jail free card.

Ann says she's now happier than she's ever been. In her first year of freedom she felt euphoric; no responsibilities except for herself. She's single and loving her life of freedom and possibilities. Ann is doing the work to put her past firmly in the past. She's opening her heart to a new kind of love relationship – a true partnership. That is indeed a happy ending for now. Ann's life as a beautiful, intelligent, powerful woman is blossoming. (If you are a single, enlightened man, contact me for a possible introduction to this fabulous woman).

I asked Ann for some parting advice for you. Here's what she had to say:

"When dating, discuss important life issues and decisions. Have conversations beyond the everyday trivial details of life. Discuss future plans for careers, raising children, and sharing family responsibilities.

"When someone tells you who he is - believe him He will never change. You can only change yourself.

"When it comes to love relationships, you cannot ride your whole life on chemistry."

Myth Five

LOVE HURTS

The musical rock group, Nazareth had a famous song with this very title, ***Love Hurts***. Since the lyrics were so popular, this song was recorded by many other artists including Cher, Boy George, Bon Jovi, and Joan Jett, to name a few. For all lovers of music, you know how easy it is to sing along, reciting the words until they become imprinted in our consciousness. We even begin to believe what we're hearing and singing to be true. Repetition and popularity play a role in this seemingly innocent programming. Combine this experience with dysfunctional role models of love and marriage from our childhood, and we have a recipe for acceptance of a belief that doesn't serve us.

Read the following excerpt of the song lyrics from ***Love Hurts*** and think about how often you've heard similar sentiments and perhaps believe them.

Love hurts, love scars, love wounds and mars
Any heart not tough or strong enough
Take a lot of pain, take a lot of pain
Love is like a cloud and it holds a lot of rain

Love is like a stove it burns you when it's hot

Some fools rave, of happiness, of blissfulness, togetherness
Oh, some fools they fool themselves, I guess....
Love is just a lie and it's made to make you blue

You may be reminded of countless other song lyrics with similar messages. There must be a reason there are thousands of songs about love, hurt, frustration and disappointment. Of course, unrequited love is painful, as most of us know from experience or certainly from friends and family who've shared their pain and agony over love gone awry. Betrayal or loneliness from the absence of a love relationship doesn't hurt any less. We embrace this love-pain connection precisely because we have experienced it as truth in our own lives.

Role models from our family marriages have significant influence for us about the love-pain connection. Think about your own paradigms of love, marriage and hurt, pain or disappointment. Most of us experienced at least some level of dysfunctional relationship during our childhood. Adults who fail to respectfully communicate their feelings and issues in the presence of children are modeling an unsustainable union. Children learn from watching others. What did you take away from your childhood experiences of love? Is there something you want to unlearn or re-frame?

My first marriage taught me a great deal about accepting old ideas and programming about love and marriage. It took me years to awaken to my plight of an unhappy, unfulfilling marriage, fraught with suffering, disappointment and pain. Until I realized this was not the common experience of well-matched happy couples, I floundered in my attempts to fix what was unrepairable. It takes two people to form the bond of relationship or marriage, and it takes those same two people committed to righting what is wrong.

I believed if I just tried hard enough, my marriage would improve. When that didn't happen, I pushed myself harder and harder to accept the inevitable while also continuing to work at it with even more resolve. All this effort produced mental and physical exhaustion, but no improvement in the marriage. It was as if I was paddling a canoe upstream while my husband was busy dragging both arms in the water to thwart any progress. Finally I woke up, jumped out and swam to shore, saving myself from certain destruction.

I hope you take time to think about your childhood imprints and experiences with the love-pain connection. How has this affected your love relationship or marriage? Are you discouraged by what you think or feel is an inevitable scenario of love causing pain and misery? Embracing the idea that love cannot exist without pain may be a central theme in your story. If so, I encourage you to read on and discover another paradigm. It is possible to be in a passionate love relationship without painful dysfunction.

As you read from my story earlier in the book, I didn't think truly happy, satisfying marriages existed. I thought discontent, disappointment and frustration with a spouse and resulting bad relationship was par for the course, as they say. I wrote this book to share a new paradigm; this does not have to be your reality.

When two people are "substantially compatible," their partnership is joyful - not painful. Shifting this old programming will free you to experience an entirely different world in relationships.

Yes, love hurts when you are with the wrong partner. Love hurts when your partner lacks respectful, open communication skills. Love hurts when feelings and issues are ignored and swept under the rug. Love hurts when you don't speak up or stand up for yourself. Love hurts when you give your all and your partner does not reciprocate. Love hurts when you try to make a relationship work, even though it wasn't right from the beginning. Love hurts when you morph into someone you aren't just to please another. Love hurts when you give up your feelings, desires and needs for another.

Once I awakened to the concept of marriage as an equal, loving, supportive partnership between two "substantially compatible" people, I knew "love hurts" would be relegated to the scrap heap of old discarded beliefs, or as I call them, outdated Marriage Myths. I hope you'll join the ranks of the deliriously happy couples who expect their love relationship to be balanced to the side of easy-flowing, respectful love and support for one another. Doesn't that sound immeasurably better?

The *Law of Attraction* teaches us we are going to receive what we think about, what we believe, and what we expect. Once I jettisoned the love-pain paradigm, my life changed quickly and dramatically. I no longer gave any energy to my past experience of love. I decided love would be whatever I agreed to accept. My decision to expect only the highest and best from love and my love partnership changed my life. Shifting your love relationship beliefs can change your life too!

Think about your childhood programing as you read Briana's story. You'll see just how dramatically her marriage was affected by her childhood role models and experiences. You'll also learn from her challenges and ultimate redemption that it's never too late to fall deeply in love with a "substantially compatible" partner and begin the life of your dreams. She didn't know it or even believe in it, but the overarching principle of the *Universe* – the *Law of Attraction* changed her life.

Briana's Story

There were hundreds of people in the cafeteria for lunch – just another ordinary day in this busy corporate office complex. Briana had no idea, that this day would be anything but ordinary. Her eyes met his in the lunch line; instantly she recognized the man she hadn't seen for thirty plus years. She hadn't even thought about him much during that time; but now seeing his familiar face in this sea of people almost caused her to stop breathing.

They'd met while in high school band camp. Briana and Liam attended different schools, and were part of the same youth organization, but saw each other infrequently. They dated a few times, once attending a Jethro Tull concert together. Sometimes they took the subway to see his father who worked at a downtown restaurant. She described Liam as very nice, respectful, kind, shy and cute. Their dates were innocent - just a sweet kiss goodnight at the door.

Briana couldn't stop thinking about him as she left the cafeteria that day. What was going on? Her mind was racing. How could they have been in the same location at the exact same time with all those other people? A few seconds earlier or later and they'd have missed each other for sure. What now? He told her he'd been in the area many times over the past few months visiting his clients. Why hadn't he contacted her? She had many questions.

Briana didn't hear from Liam again for several months. Although separated, she was not thinking about dating. Wow! She was confused. Then as suddenly as he'd appeared and then disappeared, he began calling; and they reconnected, spending hours catching up on their respective lives. Thirty plus years is a long time to cover on the phone.

Shortly thereafter he called to ask what she was doing on Sunday. He said he would like to take her to brunch. Of course she wanted to go, but he lived several hours away. Liam said he didn't mind the long drive and insisted he wanted to see her. Briana was elated - but nervous. She tried on fifteen outfits before leaving her house that afternoon.

The moment she walked into the restaurant and saw him, she began shaking like a leaf. In an instant she knew she would marry him. The emotions she felt were indescribable. Whatever had to change to make this possible would have to change. Nothing was going to block this relationship from happening. She didn't know how, and she didn't know why; but she knew in a nanosecond this was the love of her life. It was like a movie fast forwarding before her eyes – unstoppable, undeniable.

This scenario was not in her paradigm. Briana was raised by two loving parents in an environment fraught with drama. Her mother's youngest sister had lived with them for several years during Briana's early childhood. She'd married a physically abusive man. Unfortunately, young Briana was often awakened by angry conversation coming from the kitchen as her parents struggled to deal with this worsening situation. Seeing her dear aunt with bruises and black eyes was unbearable. Added to that, her father had been seriously ill for most of her parents' marriage, and he passed away when Briana was only seventeen. She was devastated.

Seeing Liam after all these years was overwhelming. Briana was rocked by her unexpected reaction. She desperately needed a pause button to find her equilibrium. Intimate relationships in her life had run the gamut from chaotic and unpredictable to the relative security she had with her husband, Tim.

Briana met Tim in college. Although they liked each other right away and went out occasionally, they most often socialized with a group of friends. She thought he was smart, sweet and a cute guy to hang around with; but it wasn't love right away for her. He, however, had quickly fallen for the beautiful, witty redhead, almost from the moment they met.

By their second summer of dating, Briana had convinced herself that Tim was a wonderful man who loved her from the inception of their relationship. She began to see him in a different light, and their relationship moved from casual to serious. When Tim announced he would be moving out of state to complete his graduate work, they decided she would go as well.

Before she left to begin a new life with Tim, Liam, fresh out of college, called out of the blue and asked her to lunch. He was moving to Washington to start his business and wanted to say his good-byes. The lunch was nice – she told him about Tim and that they were moving to California. As they were leaving, Liam paused at the door of the restaurant and said, "I'm going to marry you one day." She laughed, and they went their separate ways.

With this comment long forgotten, Briana and Tim were married and spent the next twenty-five years together. While Briana wanted to report this union had been a happy, satisfying one, it was not to be. As much as she loved Tim, his childhood emotional trauma would not be quieted. Their strong intellectual compatibility could not overcome serious deficits in other areas of intimacy. Their marriage slowly eroded one day at a time, one fit of anger and defensive reaction at a time, and one emotionally distant moment at a time. Decades of effort could not put the pieces back together again.

Briana, stunned by this sudden shift in her life after seeing Liam again, thought she could forget her experiences with him. Everything would be easier if she could put him out of her mind – or would it? What would this do to Tim? Although they'd separated, the divorce hadn't been finalized. She loved him and knew just how emotionally fragile he was. The subsequent mental gymnastics she put herself through would not prevail.

What she felt for Liam was real – probably the most real feeling she'd experienced in years. When she looked at him, she felt she was seeing his true character – his heart and soul. Being with Liam affected every cell of her body. This feeling was beyond anything she'd previously experienced. There was no denying it.

Briana sensed she'd been in a long drought, and now she had tasted the fountain of life. It was then that she realized the vast hole she'd been in with her first marriage. It was deeper and wider than she'd ever imagined. Until now she had no idea just how unsatisfying her marriage had been. No denial now – no way to turn away from Liam. No matter how hard she tried, she could not strip this experience from her consciousness.

Liam knew it too. He'd been too scared to contact her after their meeting in the cafeteria. Instead he'd sit for hours in the hallway, just hoping she'd walk by. When this didn't happen, he could no longer stop himself from hearing her voice again and he began calling. Life can be complicated and challenging, but he could not stay away. He didn't know how thirty plus years could have gone by so quickly, but it didn't matter anymore. He recalled his statement from so long ago – "I'm going to marry you one day."

Briana says she's had many "aha moments" since re-connecting with Liam. Loyalty can be a valuable attribute in a relationship, but her approach had been unhealthy. She thought the disagreements and missing intimacies with Tim were just part of marriage and that somehow things would get better with time. Besides, she believed there was nothing she could do about it. With no parents and no children, she was fearful of being alone. Tim was her best friend – how could she leave him completely alone? He had family, but their lack of closeness cancelled out any real benefits.

As a young woman, her mother had been engaged to a lawyer, but she left him for an uneducated man with few resources. For twenty-five of their forty-two years together, Briana's father had been consistently ill. Briana's mother stayed – there were happy times, but she was also sad and stressed much of her married life. The love-pain connection was clear, reinforced by her aunt who'd married a nice man only to leave him for an emotionally and physically abusive man. Was this a lesson in loyalty trumping love?

Although Briana wanted to stay married and grow old with Tim, there were just too many missing intimacies between them. As the "aha moments" continued, Briana remembered many years of wistful thinking about her ideal love match. She allowed herself to imagine the love of her life – he was out there somewhere. While she didn't necessarily believe it was possible, she visualized it happening anyway.

Visualizing your heart's desires coming true is one of the most powerful tools any person can employ. This is how the *Law of Attraction* works to manifest your dreams. Briana imagined her true love with an unaccustomed depth of feeling, unaware she was attracting that very experience. Just like gravity, we don't have to believe it exists for it to work.

Over the tumultuous years with Tim, she convinced herself their problems weren't serious enough to leave. She became a master of denial, sugar-coating their issues. She surmised other couples must have problems as well, all the while sweeping his unacceptable behavior under the proverbial rug.

Briana came to believe she must deserve Tim's blow-ups. She learned to accept his treatment of her as she escaped to more and more work outside their home. With enough activities to distract her from the reality of her tense relationship, their serious dysfunction morphed one day at a time into their new normal. She would soon learn a new definition of normal.

Liam and Briana were at the airport ready to board their plane for a week on a lovely Caribbean island. In her haste to finish work and get to the airport, she forgot her passport. Calmly they made plans for a later flight while Briana drove home to find it. With only a short window to return to the airport, Briana grabbed the first passport she found in her dresser. Now standing in line at the gate waiting to board, the bad news was delivered from the attendant – this was an expired passport. There would be no flight for them that day.

Briana said her reaction to this news was visceral. She felt panic arise as she recoiled into her body, waiting for the impending verbal assault. This is what would have happened if she'd been with Tim. They consistently fought before every trip. Tim routinely yelled, occasionally calling her names when anything went wrong. He had limited capacity for calmly handling any crisis – small or large. In this moment Briana's body reacted instinctively, expecting an imminent verbal assault.

She wanted to cry with relief as Liam took control and gently let her know it wasn't necessary to get upset: it was time to calmly focus on a solution. They would simply go back to her house, find the right passport, and fly to their destination the next morning. This is how mature, loving couples would handle the situation. Recriminations don't solve anything when there is an unanticipated problem. Yes, they would miss a day of their vacation, but no lasting harm was done.

Briana learned quite a bit that day and fell more deeply in love with Liam, if that was even possible. Tim had frequently been volatile, quick to shout and lose his temper, blaming anyone but himself for what had impinged on his expectations. Liam had reacted in such an opposite way, Briana was shocked. Of course, she felt like an idiot for this mistake, and she certainly didn't need anyone loudly calling her names. What a welcome revelation!

Briana and Liam are happily engaged and planning a wedding in the near future. They embody the definition of a loving, supportive couple. When Briana allowed herself to daydream or imagine her perfect love match, she was actually placing her order with the *Universal Creative Energy Source,* or *Spirit* – use whatever word or words work for you. This is the same energy that takes the carrot seed and makes the carrot. It's a power for creating good, and you can use it too!

When I asked Briana for some advice for you, here's what she had to say:

"Having a strong degree of intellectual intimacy with a good person does not mean the relationship is good enough for a marriage. When spiritual, physical, and/or emotional intimacy are lacking, the marriage may not survive.

"Childhood imprints, reinforced by unacceptable behaviors, last longer than you think they will. Recognize destructive behaviors for what they are and take action to save your mind, body and soul. Denial doesn't work.

"I didn't share my concerns or make any demands in my first marriage out of fear of his emotional reactions. This was a mistake I had to learn the hard way - through years of painful interactions. Don't let this happen to you. Stand up for yourself and share your needs from the beginning.

"Having the love of your life is so possible – I know that now. *P.S. A fabulous Love Coach told me that long before I believed it"*

Chapter Fifteen

Relationship Realities

Now that we've covered some of the most common relationship myths, let's examine relationship realities and advice from women who are living their ideal love life. I invite you to consider each possibility. This list is not intended to be all-inclusive. It's what I've experienced and have come to learn for myself. It represents the collective wisdom of the many women I interviewed. Take what resonates with you and leave the rest.

Use this advice as a place to begin dialogue on a topic not often discussed between women. Many of the women interviewed said no one had talked with them about love relationships. We all had to learn our lessons the hard way. Some lessons have to be learned that way, but only if you're stubborn.

If you're willing to learn from others and avoid unnecessary and costly mistakes, the following advice about love relationships and marriage is for you. Since this information is from women who have the love of their lives, chances are, their advice can help you find your love connection and build a long-term happy relationship.

I decided to include this information in my book because many women I spoke with felt confused on the subject of attracting and sustaining a love relationship. With the misguided myths you've just read about in the previous chapter, I decided it was time to provide real advice from love relationships that are thriving. You may even be inspired to add your own thoughts and ideas to your repertoire of relationship wisdom.

The world is more complex than ever. Even with the mass of information available at our fingertips, real world examples are the best teachers. There are tons of theories about how to have a great love connection and marriage, but there is nothing more enlightening than learning from actual experiences in the context of an intimate relationship. As I said earlier in the book, I hope you'll want to try these relationship realities out for yourself.

"Truly intimate and fulfilling partnerships flow naturally and easily."

I once kept this belief a secret, thinking I was the only one who thought this way. Part of me considered it was more of a wish than a reality. Once I completed the research for the book, I knew this was the type of relationship I'd longed for, but didn't know was possible until I met the love of my life. Talking with so many happily coupled women and having discovered this truth through my personal experience, I can confidently share this insight with you.

The women interviewed used terms like, "most comfortable relationship I've ever been in, easy flowing, and relaxing," to describe the relationship with the love of their life. This relationship reality is the opposite of one of the myths described in the last chapter – marriage is hard work.

Never having a serious disagreement or argument is unrealistic, but the balance should always be tipped in favor of ease in a love relationship. This concept was so new to me; I could hardly believe it was possible. My experiences of marriage, both my own first marriage and others' marriages, led me to quite the opposite conclusion. Marriage seemed more like something to be endured – a gauntlet of sorts that if run well would result in the ultimate prize.

Now that I'd jettisoned my painful, unrepairable first marriage, I was living this new reality every day. My heart was no longer heavy and my whole body felt lighter and healthier. I had what I once thought was the mythical unicorn in the forest – a genuine supportive partnership. Wow! I remain in awe of its existence, treasuring my husband and our relationship like the precious gift that it is.

You may have experienced relationships that did not uplift and lovingly support you. What I want you to know for sure is this does not have to be your reality. While I believe strongly in marriage and in putting in the effort to fix a broken relationship, I know from personal experience not everything is repairable. One person attempting to fix a two person union simply isn't workable.

As individuals, we can change ourselves and possibly influence our partner, but no one corrects our unacceptable behaviors unless we first truly desire the change for ourselves. When a man says he'll change for you, he may have good intentions; but his actions over time are the ultimate test of his resolve. An easy, flowing love relationship is possible.

"It takes two for a successful long-term partnership, but only one to destroy it."

This particular relationship reality almost didn't make it into the book. I struggled with writing this section because most of us have been taught something quite different. We've all heard the old sayings that pronounce the opposing view. We've been told since childhood sentiments like, "It takes two to tango," and "Both people in a relationship have to take responsibility for what went wrong." This sounds reasonable and logical, and I actually agree with this advice, most of the time.

My argument with this philosophy that both people are equally responsible for the demise of a marriage is that it's not always true. It takes only one person in a partnership to embezzle the money and destroy the business. It only takes one person in a love relationship to check out and refuse to discuss the issues. Yes, those who've experienced the fatal relationship detour in action might have become aware and taken action sooner, but the outcome would not necessarily have changed.

One common scenario plays out when the wife repeatedly tries to express the desire for changes in the relationship or suggests marriage counseling, but her requests are denied either through clear refusals or benign neglect. When a woman finally says it's over, it's not uncommon for her mate to suggest marriage counseling – the very thing she's pleaded for all along.

Love relationships, by definition, require the participation and cooperation of two people. The unraveling begins when one person takes responsibility for most of the activities that support the relationship, without the full participation of the partner. When this repeatedly happens, the relationship becomes unbalanced. Over time, the unbalanced weight takes its toll. Recovery is not always possible.

For example, when one person abandons his/her role as partner and becomes exclusively the "taker," the relationship is finished. Modern women are far less likely to sign-up for lifelong relationship servitude without some level of reciprocity. If you are the only "giver," you're not in a partnership. A journey through life's ups and downs is best accomplished by an evenly united pair. So remember, it's critical to address any detours from the four pillars of intimacy before they become the undoing of your love relationship or marriage.

"Working hard is something you do together to face life's challenges, not something required to sustain the relationship."

My awakening to this possibility came not with a sudden jolt, but rather through a gradual prickling of my consciousness - just one moment in time after another until my discomfort could no longer be ignored. My usual resolve and determination to make my first marriage work in spite of his apparent apathy could no longer withstand the strain of so much work.

As much as I wanted to exceed expectations in every role: daughter, mother, wife, career professional, chef, housekeeper, lawn care specialist, house painter, party planner, and financial wizard, etc., this "do it all" strategy was unsustainable. Working hard to build a better life for my family was not the problem. What I couldn't bear was the denigration of my efforts and the soul-sucking absence of loving support on any level: emotional, physical, intellectual or spiritual.

Girlfriends tried to convince me something was terribly wrong with my marriage. They could see and feel my misery. And readers, here's the real danger – accepting a dysfunctional lifestyle over time makes "normal" indiscernible. I actually thought most marriages were fraught with similar struggles and devoid of reciprocity. As I began to awaken to my dire situation, it became clear that most of my friends were in loving, supportive relationships that had no resemblance to mine.

Simple things like flowers for special occasions, celebrating romantic occasions such as Valentine's Day and anniversaries, kisses to welcome me home after a day at work or a business trip – all missing. I was doing all the work to sustain our home, children and couple's relationship. All this hard work left me exhausted and negatively impacted my health. Love relationships and marriage are meant to be life affirming and joyous. Slowly the light returned for me.

Consistently working hard and struggling to sustain a relationship most likely means you are not with the right person. This may be difficult to hear and accept, but it's the truth. I wouldn't have had the courage to write about this if it weren't for my experience and the hundreds of women who confirmed it. Many of us worked hard, struggling unsuccessfully to make our first marriages work, but now enjoy loving, supportive relationships that flow with ease. Don't accept less.

"Substantial compatibility is a key ingredient for a sustainable relationship."

One of my college roommates once told me her parents never went to bed at the same time. This arrangement may well have worked for them and perhaps even countless others, but it may also be an indicator of incompatibility on other levels. One of the great joys of romantic companionship or marriage is being together at the end of the day, cuddling, kissing and sleeping together.

This example may not resonate with you, but hopefully the point is clear. To have "substantial compatibility" with your mate means you share more common goals, values, activities and plans than not. Think about a love relationship that didn't work out and make a checklist of areas in which you were incompatible and those you had in common. Which list is longer?

While not sharing bedtime is a big deal for some, your list may be quite different. And some things matter more than others. For example, not sharing tastes in food may be inconsequential or can cause friction in otherwise enjoyable activities such as cooking, dining out, and vacation planning. You can decide what is important for you and in what areas compromise works.

Dating your opposite personality type can be fun and interesting, but at some point in the relationship, another's opposing preferences and habits usually become annoying. Having "substantial compatibility" brings harmony and helps create a foundation for the relationship to thrive, rather than become stuck in unnecessary conflict. No one agrees on everything in a relationship, so creating balance that's tipped to the side of shared likes is the key.

Having experienced the contrast between "substantially compatible and substantially incompatible" relationships, I can without any hesitation say the former is highly preferred. Time spent compromising, arguing, feeling the frustration of disagreements, large and small, can siphon the vitality out of a relationship. Sharing mutually agreed upon plans, goals and values makes working out small or inconsequential problems more bearable.

I encourage you to think about what's important for you to thrive in a "substantially compatible" love relationship. In other words, don't look for love on the golf course if you don't want to play or become a weekend "golf widow."

"It's not about giving up your freedom; it's about being truly free to be yourself."

To be loved and appreciated for what you bring to your love relationship is a magnificent experience. Anyone who demands change to your true essence or belittles your passions is not in love with you. When a potential life partner makes changing who you are a priority, he is waving a red flag of warning that this match is not for you. One of the great joys of love and marriage is being appreciated and accepted for your unique abilities and qualities.

This lesson took years for me to learn. My stubbornness and intense desire to make my marriage work ultimately failed. I was unable to be myself or pursue my own interests without a constant barrage of negativity and criticism. When someone you love continually chooses to put his needs and desires ahead of yours, it'll always be at your expense.

True partnership, the definition of modern marriage, is about reciprocity. That means each person should be free to explore his/her interests, hobbies and passions, with the full support of his/her partner. The more you have in common, the less you'll be asked to compromise in a love relationship. Of course, you'll have differences with your mate, but they will not be serious enough to unbalance your love relationship.

Modern marriage is like a pliable vessel, supporting and sustaining each person in the union. By definition, modern marriage means freedom to evolve and grow together. Any attempts to significantly change the other person or demand conformity with another's wishes negates the purpose of being together. After many years of feeling confined and disrespected as a person, I finally realized old ideas of marriage as lifelong bondage were not workable.

Regardless of your previous paradigms, I hope you will embrace this concept and know for sure that a man who really loves you will not try to control you. He will revel in who you are. He'll be your biggest cheerleader. He'll want what's best for you. Both partners can enjoy immense freedom and passion in a modern marriage if they approach their relationship expecting nothing less.

"Passion has the fragility of a delicate flower – if neglected, it will die."

It's very easy to fall into routines and put the romance on the back burner. In the same way that a beautiful and delicate flowering plant needs the right soil, water and sunlight, a love relationship requires nurturing as well. Most of us weren't taught how to do this, and we were not aware of the importance of sustaining a loving partnership or marriage. We may even have witnessed a myriad of dysfunctional behaviors from adults during our childhood.

Fortunately, I did have a few good role models which allowed me to learn about how couples could love, support, and respect each other as romantic partners - even after raising children and years of marriage. I didn't think much about it until I discovered romance had slowly disappeared from my first marriage. Our relationship slid one day at a time into mutual toleration- not a recipe for happily ever after.

Keeping romance alive in a love relationship and marriage is so important for each person's overall happiness and satisfaction. With good role models often missing and open discussion in even shorter supply, it's not surprising how often lack of passion affects our most intimate of relationships. Just like any other marital issue, denial doesn't work. The longer a couple continues without having an honest conversation about their individual needs, the deeper and more unresolvable the problems become.

Remember that love connections erode slowly, one day at a time, one gesture or absence of conversation at a time. My husband and I agreed early in our relationship to honor our true feelings by regularly sharing them with each other without boundaries. This agreement has been a revelation and much like a deep breath of fresh air for both of us, since we were unaccustomed to this way of being in a relationship. After a decade of marriage, we know it can't work any other way for us.

My research confirmed the happiest of couples choose to continue dating and bringing romance into their everyday lives – regardless of the years they've been together. It's not complicated. It's a choice. Decide today that when you have the love of your life, you will keep your passion alive throughout the years. How you do that will change and evolve over time, but don't let your lover turn into just a roommate. During my interviews, one woman confided she was her husband's wife, girlfriend, and mistress all rolled into one. This same attitude also applies for men.

"We care for and respect what we truly cherish."

We didn't have expensive or fancy furnishings in my childhood home, but what we did have was a very smart mother who shared her valuable lessons with us. Each spring and again in the fall my sisters and I were required to participate in a thorough seasonal house cleaning. While I'm sure this project was not on the top of my desired activities list, I, nevertheless, fondly remember those days. I didn't know it then, but I was learning more than cleaning techniques.

My mother instilled in us the values of teamwork, cleanliness, and something equally important – respect for our home and the things that allowed us to live in relative comfort. Sloppiness was not tolerated. Every piece of furniture was removed from the room, polished and returned only after the room was cleaned from top to bottom. Every accessory, large and small, was given its particular brand of cleaning. Our belongings, moderate as they were, had the best of care because our finances made these items irreplaceable.

I share this story, not to equate love relationships with worldly possessions, but to illustrate the point that we tend to care for what we truly cherish. Many women and men are able to attract potential partners, but then they forget to nourish and support these relationships, taking for granted the partner they have chosen. Relationships can also suffer from benign neglect. What can you do to prevent this from happening to your potential love relationship?

Set an intention and make a plan to tend your relationship with as much care as you would your home or garden. Spend quality time together, plan to keep dating after the wedding ceremony, talk about how you want to grow together and make a joint commitment to keep closely connected on all levels: physical, emotional, intellectual, and spiritual.

Nothing trumps spending time together sharing activities, thoughts, feelings and even the silence. Couples build strong bonds one step at a time. It's the seemingly small things that can either nurture or erode an intimate relationship. Taking care of yourself and prioritizing your partner's feelings makes handling life's bigger challenges possible.

"Shouting at your partner is self-indulgent. Over time, it creates scars that may never heal."

Even well adjusted, balanced, and generally optimistic people become angry or frustrated once in a while. It's human to respond emotionally when things don't go according to our plans. As with the previous advice, it is not okay to take anger out on anyone else. Being upset with a loved one, even if there is good cause, isn't a license to shout at him/her No one hears you when you're screaming anyway.

If you really want to be heard, discuss differences when you can rationally do so. Think about how you'd like to receive feedback from your partner. How do you feel when someone shouts in anger at you? Instead of reserving best behaviors for colleagues, friends, and strangers, remember it's equally important to treat family with respect.

The common belief that marriage should be a safe place to express ourselves has been used unwisely to defend outbursts of ranting and raving. Emotionally mature, couples know better. They realize the long-term effects of directing uncontrolled anger at their spouse or partner. The harm that results is like a repetitive wound that eventually leaves a scar. Learning to appropriately channel anger is non-negotiable for a happy, sustainable love relationship.

Since appropriate expression of strong emotions like anger probably wasn't the topic of conversation at the dinner table or any other time during our childhoods, most of us likely learned a few bad habits. Screaming, swearing, hitting anything - even inanimate objects - and/or name calling are not in the appropriate or respectful category. This type of behavior is always unacceptable. The one exception - the ranting maniac is alone in the woods or in the middle of nowhere. Then I think it is okay to let it out, if you really must.

Instead, when foul tempers, crankiness, and other unpleasant attitudes are brought home to those we love, a time-out may save the day. Our family deserves our very best. Therefore, if you're in bad humor, tell your partner and let everyone know you'll be in your room or taking a hot bath until you've recovered enough to be social. Find a productive way to calm yourself. You will not regret taking time to center yourself, but you will likely regret words spoken in anger.

"Don't make a habit of kissing frogs unless you want to get warts."

Though we can't really get warts from kissing a frog, this old cliché illustrates a point. You cannot change a broken man into the whole and happy man of your dreams – no matter how much you love him. It can be tempting to think you are the exception and your tender loving care is just what's needed to change this work in progress into a masterpiece. It won't work. You can cry about it, you can be mad about it; but it won't change the truth.

Why not raise your standards? You may have heard the saying, "We teach people how to treat us." While I'm not one to have regrets, I do wish I'd known this many years ago. Had I heard and understood this concept, my years of toleration for unacceptable behaviors would have been significantly shorter or perhaps non-existent. I'm not a big fan of suffering. I hope you agree and commit yourself to requiring respectful treatment at all times.

I hope this book has helped you discern what you will and will not accept in your life, especially from someone you're dating. When a possible future partner wants to spend time with you, he needs to be worthy of your time and attention. Be ready to identify a person who's not up to your standards. Don't give him the opportunity to disrespect you in any way. There really are many fish in the sea, so to speak. You don't have to date every person that expresses an interest in you.

No, frogs do not turn into princes with even your sweet kiss. A frog will always be a frog. You want a prince – the prince that's perfect for you. Notice I didn't say the perfect man – I said the one perfect for you. That's a very different request. Since no one is perfect, you can relax and stop searching for unattainable perfection.

Yes, there is training to be done in love partnerships, but don't settle for a fix-it project unless you can handle the disappointment. Know what your relationship deal breakers are and hold to them. Physically or verbally abusive men, alcoholic or drug addicted men, deceitful, dishonest men or criminals are always on the deal breakers list. What's on your personal deal breakers list? Don't you deserve to have a love partner who strives for excellence in every area of his life?

"You can only wear the wrong size shoes for so long before you get a bunion or worse."

Jamie Roberts

I love this practical advice from my friend! We can all readily relate to this type of discomfort. Everyone has experienced painful shoe days. No matter how much you stretch them or tamper with their construction, they still won't feel good on your feet. That's the truth about wrong partners, as well. It's best to wait for the right fit.

Yes, but you really love them (the shoes) or him (your prospective love match). With a little stretching or training, the fit might be perfect. I know this is what we've all thought about and probably tried, whether it was the shoes or the man. Sometimes this strategy works with shoes, but rarely will struggling to force a love match work out in the end. A man may yield under pressure for a while for a variety of reasons, but the poor fit will eventually manifest.

So what's a woman to do in the meantime? Be open to dating and learn to reserve judgement on the fit until you get to know the real person behind the façade of initial dating. Yes, this takes time and patience; but like savoring a good cheese and fine wine, rushing doesn't contribute to the final outcome. Letting a love relationship develop naturally over time will give you critical information about the potential for long-term relationship success with that particular person.

As with shoes, you'll learn which type suits you best as you experience more styles. Women who have no prior dating experience or serious relationship history for comparison are more likely to latch onto their first opportunities too early in the process. Becoming a discerning shopper requires time, experience, and a set of standards. You don't want just any black dress shoe, you want the one that feels comfortable from the beginning and makes you feel beautiful and desirable. The new shoes must compliment your wardrobe and distinct style. Ask yourself this question: Does he complement my life?

Remember that you may be able to return or throw away a pair of ill-fitting shoes, but separating from or ending a marriage you've devoted years to developing is much more difficult and heartbreaking. The right fit is waiting for you. In the meantime you may need to learn more about what makes your perfect match. When that ideal partner or pair of shoes shows up, you'll recognize the worth of waiting, instead of settling.

"You may be lonely without a partner, but if you marry the wrong person you'll experience true loneliness."

Most of us understand and accept the reality of being by ourselves from time to time. We know what to expect, and hopefully we've cultivated the skill of appreciating our own company. When we're alone, we have no expectations of engaging in conversation or activities with someone who isn't physically present, unless we're talking on the telephone. Being alone can sometimes feel lonely, but loneliness doesn't have to be the predominant state of mind. Expectations in this circumstance are regulated by the normalcy of the situation – everyone experiences being alone at times.

Moving from being single to becoming part of a couple changes our expectations of how much time we'll actually spend alone. Couples talk, plan, cook, shop, sleep and maybe even work or vacation together. Loneliness is relegated to the past. This is the common understanding most of us have on the subject of sharing our lives in love and marriage. But what happens when this scenario begins to unravel?

There are many ways for a love relationship or marriage to die. This concept changed my paradigm forever when I stopped long enough to discover its truth. My epiphany – hey wait a minute, I'm married! Why do I feel so lonely? Women often share their similar experiences with me. Just because someone is physically present doesn't mean the partnership is healthy or thriving. This once fully engaged intimate partner may no longer be present on any other level. Communication may have ceased or become stifled – intellectually, emotionally and/or spiritually.

Learning to discern the difference between a slight detour in communication with your would-be husband or wife and a total mismatch is important. I encourage you to take time to assess the level of compatibility you enjoy with your potential mate. Of course, as life proceeds, there will be detours from our ideal standards. Course corrections are easier to accomplish when both partners are committed to maintaining consistent respectful communication.

When a couple has serious issues in any of the four pillars of intimacy before the wedding, it's time to re-asses the viability of the union. Taking time now may be the best prevention to experiencing the deep loneliness of being the only person present in the partnership.

"You must have the qualities you want to attract."

A friend once told me that her single aunt, who was quite overweight, with no care for her appearance and unable to keep a job often remarked that she was going to find a handsome, rich, hunk of a man to marry. That's not likely to happen. This woman is living in a state of delusion, content with a fantasy life and unwilling to take steps towards her stated goals. In other words, she isn't willing to develop the qualities she desires in a mate.

If you want a healthy, kind, generous, and respectful partner who takes care of himself physically, spiritually, and financially, you'll need to have those qualities to offer as well. Spending time crying about this truth or refusing to recognize the power of the *Law of Attraction* is wasted time. The good news is you don't need to take anyone else's word for it – you can prove it for yourself.

If you haven't done so already, I encourage you to put together a list of the qualities you're seeking in a mate. Then ask yourself how many of these qualities you have in sufficient quantity to be satisfied. Happy, loving, supportive people who take care of themselves physically, emotionally and financially are generally not attracted to their opposites in these categories.

While there is plenty of controversy surrounding the question of what creates attraction between two individuals, my experience and research supports the basic tenets of the *Law of Attraction* or put simply - that which is like unto itself attracts the essence of the same. Why not take the time to develop the higher values and qualities of the life you'd love to be sharing with another?

Striving for excellence or as Oprah says "living your highest and best life" is the fastest and best way I know of to find yourself in the company of others you'd like to spend time with and get to know. By now you've read the stories of women who've connected with the love of their life, sometimes after struggling through relationships that did not uplift and support them. It's easy to become stuck in the self-pity mode instead of learning the lessons and moving forward.

What has happened in the past does not need to define your future. People can and do change and evolve, if they want to do so. Embracing joy, happiness, kindness, compassion and gratitude, to name a few, is the best way to attract more of the same. Try it out for yourself!

"Don't jump into bed with someone without a foundation of intimacy on other levels."

It's important not to confuse physical intimacy with compatibility. When a deeply intimate connection isn't joined by a true knowledge of another's essential nature, disappointment and heartache can ensue. Sexual intimacy is a special part of a healthy and whole love partnership. It's not a building block that assures a solid foundation for future growth.

Today's culture seems preoccupied with all things sexual in the absence of any context of love or respect. Sharing the precious gift of your body with another person is an act of intimacy not to be taken without thought. Physical intimacy is not a guarantee of shared mutual interests beyond the bedroom. How will you feel about tonight if he never contacts you again?

The purpose of this section is not to give a morality lesson. Your personal morality standards are up to you. What I'd like to share is some food for thought about what happens when women engage in sexual intimacy prior to establishing intimacy on other levels first. Most men will happily accept sex from a willing date, but they do not necessarily connect this activity with the concept of an exclusive love relationship or even being in a relationship at all.

This is the part women often get wrong. Having enjoyable or even great sex does not mean he thinks you are relationship material. All of the fabulous sex in the world won't change this dynamic. If a monogamous relationship is your desire, then why not wait for it? Do you think he'll go elsewhere if he isn't getting it from you? Not a chance, if he's truly interested in you. Don't you want to wait a bit to find out?

Please take time to be honest with yourself about any past experiences. Don't romanticize hook-ups for more than what they were. For a woman, trying to get to love through sex is folly. Set your own standards – don't be influenced by today's obsession with sexualizing everything. You are worthy of his time and attention to get to know you before sharing this intimate bond. Focus on what you want. If you're reading this book, you are probably seeking a deeply satisfying sustainable love relationship or marriage. While not first or second date conversation material, it's best to be honest about your goals before giving him too much of yourself.

"Life is too long to be unhappy."

We've been told since childhood that life is too short for a variety of things – anger, unhappiness, time wasting, grudge holding - and the list goes on. Many years ago, a friend relayed to me that her mother's philosophy was just the opposite - she said life was too long to be unhappy. I agree. The seconds, minutes, hours, days, months and years we spend on this planet are too long and precious to waste on unhappiness.

I hope you will take time to reflect on your personal view of life being either too short or too long for living someone else's dream. My friend's mother's philosophy made more sense to me. At the time I was suffering through years of a dysfunctional marriage that had been impossible to bring back to life. With no prospects of improvement, staying was not a viable option. I came to understand the value of spending my time claiming my happiness and associating with other like-minded people.

Choosing to leave any long-term love relationship or marriage is not easy, but neither is staying. I asked myself if I'd rather stay and be miserable for the next fifty years or bear the temporary pain of uncoupling. You may also have a choice to make. Which version of the following quote feels best for you? From an unknown author:

"Life is too short to spend time with people who suck the happiness out of you."

My version,

"Life is too long to spend time with people who suck the happiness out of you."

Deepak Chopra, famous doctor, author, speaker and new thought leader, had this to say about happiness, *"Research has shown that the best way to be happy is to make each day happy."* You can choose today to be happy regardless of your circumstances. You can choose to surround yourself with other happy people, rather than spend your life trying to make someone else happy. Another's happiness is not your job. You are only responsible for your own state of happiness.

"We always have a choice."

I spent years feeling trapped by a choice made in my youth with all the best intentions. Sure that my choice had effectively and permanently eliminated any option to choose differently, I willed myself to keep trying anyway. That ingrained belief in the finality of my choice brought me despair like nothing ever had before. Now I know I suffered needlessly.

Ask yourself, as I did, what will happen if I don't make a new choice? Will my life be enhanced or diminished by my choice to accept or reject what's happening now? When I really thought about what my life was going to be like if I stayed, I knew nothing was going to change the trajectory of my relationship. It takes both parties to effect lasting change for the better. As I said before, some things, once shattered, cannot be repaired.

That I could choose to save myself was a revelation. I wanted to berate myself for taking so long to discover this possibility. What had happened to this smart, confident Magna Cum Laude college graduate? Did I turn in my intellect for my Mrs. Degree? Right away, I stopped myself from this useless line of inquiry. No longer feeling the need to figure out "why" was a big step in the right direction. It didn't matter why or how long it took me to see the truth: it only mattered that I did.

I did have a choice and once I accepted that as my new reality, life blossomed beyond my dreams. I experienced freedom, love and joy as never before or even imagined. My new choice took all the courage I could muster. Judgement and disapproval were on the other side waiting for me to step through the door of my new choice. My decision to proceed and live my truth, regardless of what anyone else had to say about it, was the only sane decision for me.

I hope you know there's always a choice just waiting for you. You are worthy of being loved, adored, cherished and respected in all of your relationships, and above all, in your most intimate of love relationships. Know that you are the master of your destiny.

To conclude this section I want to share an essay my husband wrote twenty years ago as he was experiencing his own personal epiphany. I hope you take this message to heart and reflect on your personal choices. Our choices are the containers of infinite possibilities.

CHOICES

Many people don't realize it, but each day is made up of a series of choices. The sum of each day's choices builds a lifetime. Whether it's what clothes we will wear today, who we will marry tomorrow, or what career path we will follow the next day, each choice affects where we will be at the end of life's path.

One of the easiest choices we can make each day, many times the most profound, is the attitude in which we will embrace the day. We can't change our past as much as we may want to; we normally can't change someone else – we can only change ourselves.

In broadcasting, the instructors don't teach perfection because they know mistakes will happen – the key to success is how well we recover from a mistake. I believe it's the same with life. I agree with the sages of motivational speaking who state, "Life is ten percent what happens to you and ninety percent how you react to it."

You really do have a choice. When I came to the realization that I really did have choices in life, it changed mine dramatically. I'll say it again; you really do have a choice! Of all that God created, his greatest gift to humanity was the freedom of choice. You can choose to react to life with a positive attitude, looking for the silver lining in every cloud, or react to situations with a negative attitude, finding the worst in every situation, and then stand on the sidelines saying, "why me?"

I challenge you to choose to embrace each day with a positive attitude. Try it for at least twenty-one days, the time it takes to make or break a habit. If you don't see a marvelous change in your home and business life, then go back to the way you were. What have you got to lose but a better life?

If you don't already have a positive attitude, choosing to have one today and every day will impact your life more than anything else you could have happen to you. If you don't care where life's road leads you, choose any door and take any path because they will all lead to the same disappointing destination. However, if you want a happier and more fulfilling life, try going through the narrow door leading to the path of success with a positive attitude.

Life, as well as success, is not a destination. Both are journeys that are built on one choice at a time. Start today on the path you want by choosing to have a positive attitude. You really do have a choice!

Allan Wick
1990

Chapter Sixteen

Conclusion

Thus far we've met strong and resilient women with determination to change their own lives and the courage to share their very personal highs and lows. Without exception, these women intended to stay in their marriages for the rest of their lives. Without exception, they tried hard to make them work. When their marriages ultimately failed, they were heartbroken.

The myths you've read about relationships along with any others you've encountered need to be scrutinized and weighed against real life experiences. I encourage you to reject any commonly accepted relationship wisdom that does not feel right for you nor support your goals. While our ancestors most likely had the best intentions in sharing their wisdom with us, their relationship paradigms are very different from ours today.

For example, love partnerships are not going to thrive in an environment of ceaseless work every waking hour. Happy, sustainable marriages are not created by endless efforts to make the best of a difficult situation or through barely keeping your sanity because of vastly different values or lifestyle choices.

Having the love of your life, a deeply soul-satisfying connection, is possible for you. Not having the relationship you want or suddenly finding yourself alone doesn't mean you're forever doomed in love. Remember - you have a choice. You can choose to close your heart to love, or you can choose to set your standards and be open to the infinite possibilities for connecting with the love you desire. It's up to you.

As you read this section's concluding story you may want to think about how unquestioned acceptance of old wisdom and the absence of real information may be affecting your relationship choices. Life changed dramatically in many ways on many levels when Imani was exposed to higher thoughts and new concepts for living. As she embraced life, awakening to the truth of her own being and value, she was able to give and accept love from the heart. No longer the unwitting victim of another's uninformed and desperate choices, Imani decided to walk a different path – one of joy, authenticity, and spirituality.

"Until I fall in love with me, there will be no real healthy love relationship."

Imani

Imani's Story

While still in high school, Imani, a beautiful and talented black girl was chosen as lead singer for an all-white male community band. That was an unusual combination for the early 70's in the Midwest, but Imani loved to sing. She thoroughly enjoyed herself. It was a solace since her childhood had been prematurely disrupted by abuse, a family legacy spanning several generations.

One night while on stage, Imani looked into the audience and was instantly drawn to a boy she'd never met. She asked her cousin who he was. Later, when Imani asked her cousin to introduce them, he told her the young man had a girlfriend. Nevertheless, he introduced them. The chemistry was instantaneous.

Several weeks later, while sitting in the back seat of a car with her friends at a drive-in theater, the young man approached and began a conversation. Imani responded by letting him know she understood he had a girlfriend. He then told her his relationship with the girlfriend had ended. Walt, a gentle, loving poet, and Imani had an immediate connection.

Although she didn't fully realize it at the time, her childhood struggle with abuse made her very needy. She didn't see the signs of Walt's drug addiction. Also, it didn't help that his friends weren't happy that he was dating a Black girl. One day his mother came into his room. Upon seeing a picture of Imani she asked who that girl was. When Walt replied, "My girlfriend," his mother said in a mildly disapproving tone, "Oh that's nice," and walked away. They were young, and their relationship could not survive their personal struggles coupled with the lack of support from family and friends.

Imani moved to New York to further her music career. On occasion she returned home and often revisited the club where Walt and she first met. One evening she saw him there and they had a good time catching up on each other's lives. A year later he died of a drug overdose.

Imani searched for someone to make her feel whole and happy. She wanted someone to validate her existence. She found herself in a high profile marriage, rife with chaos and drug addiction. She stayed longer than seemed wise; but like many women, she was determined to make the best of her circumstances for herself and their two children. When she was unable to endure the situation any longer, she left. The divorce was followed by another marriage and subsequent divorce.

Upon reflection, she realized there was only one common denominator in all her life dramas. It was she. Imani finally recognized that she would keep pulling broken men in until something changed within her. Imani said, "Until I fall in love with me, there will be no real healthy love relationship." She decided she must focus on what was happening inside her that enabled these choices. What would make her feel loveable?

By that time, her children were in high school with all of their own dramas, and Imani was focused on her own path toward wholeness. Her time was spent parenting and taking spiritual development classes. She'd come a long way since her first love and ensuing heartbreaks. She knew a person can't have deep intimacy if she was not willing to show up as herself.

Imani was standing in the bookstore shortly after teaching a church program for teenagers when a man approached. He commented on how cool it was that she was engaged in working with the local teens. She vividly remembers that moment. When I asked her how she felt, she said, "My heart immediately relaxed."

Not long after, Imani was scheduled to sing in a program for the prison ministry, so security was tight for this post nine-eleven event. All the program participants were outside in the parking lot for over an hour waiting for the strict security procedures to begin. She wore an orange blouse that day. The sun shone on her just right. Stephan, the man from the bookstore, saw Imani and approached her commenting, "Wow, you look really great in this light with your orange shirt." She replied, "What? Are you a photographer?" As it turned out he was.

In the ensuing discussion Imani learned he was the author of a book of photographs. When she expressed interest in seeing it, he asked if he could call and arrange a time to show it to her. Imani knew in her heart there was another kind of love than the abusive treatment she'd received, but she hadn't yet seen nor experienced it for herself.

Several weeks later, he called. They met one afternoon, and he showed her his photographs. Love was captured in each one of them. The conversation continued through dinner. At the end of the evening, Imani asked Stephan what his intentions were. He was a little intimidated by the directness of her question. She let him know that she was not interested in marriage or bed hopping. She was looking for open communication in a healthy relationship. If all he wanted was to hang out, she wasn't participating

Imani later asked him why he had taken so long to call after their conversation in the prison parking lot. He said he knew he had to be real if he was going to make the call.

Over the next two years they had an incredible journey of "surface intimacy" as Imani describes it. At that point, she felt the need to move to another level – to have a deeper soul connection. The relationship had become static. He didn't know what she was talking about. While they were breaking up, he asked her to see a spiritual counselor with him. She agreed and they entered into counseling in hopes of finding what they'd been missing.

During the process, Imani awoke abruptly one morning at 3 a.m. She felt a hand touching her and strongly sensed his energy with another woman. She reminded herself that they were no longer a couple and so his relationship with another woman was none of her business. Still, she was deeply affected by this experience. When she brought it up in their next counseling session, Stephan said he'd met someone at an event and they'd gone hiking together. Nothing else had happened.

Imani and Stephen continued counseling – deepening their bond of intimacy. One year later, they were married. The night before the wedding, Stephan said they needed to talk because he wanted to go into the marriage completely clean. He told Imani that his story about hiking with the other woman was true, but they'd also shared a kiss.

They've been married for fifteen years in a wonderful and intense relationship. Imani says soul mates are not necessarily the easiest people with whom to grow, stretch, and love. However, they will stand in the fire with you and tell you the truth, even when you don't want to hear it. That's love.

Neither Stephan nor Imani had anyone in their lives modeling authentic love. The relationship they created was different from anything they'd ever seen or experienced. This was the first time in Imani's life she hadn't been asked to compromise her authenticity.

Her advice:

"Do not become a chameleon. Give him who you are. If he can't accept it, he is not the right one for you.

"By not showing up in authenticity, you can't be loved for who you are.

"Men tell you upfront who they really are, but we think we're so fabulous we can change them. That isn't so."

Chapter Seventeen

The Research

This book is not a dissertation; it is not a quantitative analysis nor a formal research paper. It is about the real life experiences of women who've successfully found the love of their lives, including the author; and it has been written for the many women still searching. This research included a seven question survey along with an interview about each woman's love relationship experiences.

I became keenly interested in this subject after meeting, falling in love, and marrying my second husband. The deep joy and gratitude I felt for our relationship frequently spilled into my conversations. As my interest grew, my network of female colleagues and friends expanded. What began as ordinary social networking became an attention grabber as I met more women, delighted to talk about love.

I soon discovered common threads throughout the women's stories. A few remained silent on the subject, many were still looking for love, others smiled radiantly as they told me they had the love of their life. Those conversations sparked my interest. I wanted to know more.

More specifically, I wanted to know how true love came into their lives and if their experience was different or similar to mine. As the interviews continued, it became clear. Our stories were unique, yet fundamentally the same. For some, authentic love happened the first time, but many others learned through the trials of unworkable marriages that led to divorce.

The subjects of the interviews live all over the United States and in several other countries. These love relationships ran the gamut from heart-breaking disappointments to true intimacy with a life partner. They are doctors, business women, entrepreneurs, celebrities, teachers, stay at home mothers, ministers, and international speakers. What they have in common is their belief they have the love of their life – the best and most comfortable and satisfying love relationship they've ever experienced.

When I began interviewing women for the research, I thought about my own experience and developed a set of questions designed to discover more about each woman's love relationship history. I had no expectations and strived to be as objective as possible. I wanted to know how it happened for them. I asked them where they were in their lives before, during, and after meeting the love of their lives. As the interviews progressed, I became more and more intrigued by their responses. My beliefs about finding a deep love connection were confirmed more clearly than I'd ever imagined.

I learned so much during my research, and I want to share it with you. The survey questions and short summary of the most prevalent responses are included in the next chapter. I loved hearing the stories as much as the women enjoyed sharing them. I hope you find this information as interesting and enlightening as I did.

Question 1

Were you actively looking for a partner when you met your spouse?

You may be surprised by the answers to this question. You've probably been told by a well-meaning friend or family member that if you want a partner, you'd better be out there in the dating scene competing for someone or otherwise searching for love.

Searching for a potential mate has become serious business for many singles. The Internet has expanded search options nationally and internationally. That isn't necessarily good or bad; it has widened the circle of prospects for sure. With new technology and the proliferation of Internet dating sites, one might be tempted to think there are more successful matches being made.

Without a doubt, many couples have met via those sites and have connected with the love of their lives. Two people can meet anywhere. There are as many ways to meet your mate as there are places to meet. But, there are millions of single women still looking for their life partner in spite of Internet dating services.

When I started the interviewing process, it occurred to me that I was not looking for a new partner when the man of my dreams walked into my life. I was specifically not looking and told most of my friends that I would never remarry – no matter how long I lived on this planet. I was quite sure of my position, and no one could have dissuaded me. No one that is, except the wonderful man who's now my husband.

As you've read, most of the women commented on the status of their search early in the interview. Some were so worn out by it they'd given up. Others were unhappy with the results of their quest and decided to abandon it. The more women I interviewed and asked this question, the more amazed I became. **No one was actively looking for her life partner when she met him.** The reason they weren't looking varied, but the answers were all the same. What an interesting similarity between these now happily coupled women! Think about this result and evaluate what it might mean for you. Make the decision to take a recess from the search.

Question 2

When did you know he was the one?

I asked this question primarily because of the immediacy of my own knowing. I knew within three weeks of meeting my husband that he was the one for me. There was no complicated decision making process or endless deliberation.

Not everyone understands the depth of her connection at the same time as her future partner. Others are not fully aware of the possibilities for a love connection that may be right in front of them until much later. Whenever it happens will be unique for you and your partner. Most of the interviewees confirmed they knew early in the relationship. The long-term commitment or marriage may have been months or years away, but the clarity around the future longevity of the relationship was astonishingly rapid.

Some of the answers to this question are listed below:

- *After two months when he was out of town for the first time*
- *On our third date*
- *Within six weeks*
- *Instantly after talking to him*
- *Within the first sixty days of being together after a long distance romance*
- *The night I met him*
- *As soon as I realized I couldn't wait to talk to him*
- *Within weeks of meeting him*
- *When I really listened to my heart and opened my eyes*

Question 3

How did you know he was the one?

It didn't seem helpful to say, I just knew. The "knowing" was central to the message from every woman: and as the interviews progressed, the pattern emerged. No one thought about or made a list of pros and cons for the relationship in order to decide they were a perfect match. The women were informed about the character of their potential mates from witnessing their actions. Trust evolved as the relationship progressed.

External behavior is the clearest indicator of how someone really feels. Getting to know the person always preceded the women's commitment. Knowing he was "the one," was confirmed over time as the character that was sensed became realized by demonstrated behaviors. Taking time to learn about and see for oneself the true essence of a person's heart, created the solid ground upon which to grow.

As you will see from the following list of answers from the interviewees, all of them responded to the questions from their personal experiences. Their answers are unique, but also similar. How they knew came from their heart – from that deep feeling of well-being and peace that they experienced in the presence of their beloved. No one did extensive soul-searching about it. No one said it was the result of struggle or hard work.

If either person has hesitation around the rightness of the partnership, the union is wrong for both parties. Most of us have fallen for someone in our lifetime who did not return our affections. While it is unpleasant to have our heart broken, it's worse when it happens after years of hope or decades of marriage. Only love reciprocated brings true joy and soul-satisfying intimacy.

Some of the answers to this question are listed below:

- *The relationship was so easy; it was filled with joy and happiness*
- *He was interested in my life and I in his in ways that complemented each other*
- *We had the same values and could talk endlessly*
- *He was really there for me in every way*
- *The built in comfort level*

- *How I felt when I was with him*
- *There were so many things we had in common, including our values*
- *He was so warm and caring*
- *When I found him standing at the door with a rose*
- *I knew this was how it was going to be*
- *I allowed my knowing to direct my thinking*
- *It was the feeling – nothing logical*
- *How at ease we were with each other; trust and love were given so freely*
- *His love was so pure and genuine – I'd never felt that before*

Question 4

Was it your heart's desire to have a spouse/significant other?

By asking this question, I primarily wanted to know if having a partner was an expressed desire prior to meeting their ideal partner. There weren't any no's to this question. ***Every woman said it was her heart's desire to have the love of her life*** – to be loved most deeply and completely. Some had pushed their desire into the recesses of their memory, as I had, thinking it really didn't exist. The lesson: when the head relinquishes control to the heart, what we've been hoping and praying for can happen.

All of the women sent positive energy to this desire – feeling it, visualizing it, but not always thinking it would or could happen. Co-creation with the *Universal Creative Energy Source* works from the wholeness of our desires. Merely thinking about what we want usually brings more wanting – more acknowledgement of lack. Wanting all by itself can block the manifestation of our desires.

Experiencing the "feeling" that you already have what you desire is the secret to receiving. Feeling moves us from head to heart where the real magic unfolds. I loved seeing the faces of the women change as they affirmatively answered this question.

Question 5

Please complete the following sentence: It was love at first ________________.

Asking this question was fun. I wanted to know the intimate details. I never thought much about this type inquiry until it happened in my life. On several occasions, my husband and I've been asked this very question from perfect strangers while having dinner in a restaurant. Apparently, we seemed extraordinarily happy prompting the question, "Was it love at first sight?" My husband always answers right away with, "No, it was love at first kiss." I love his swift sweet answer. I knew it was love at first kiss as well, but hadn't thought about it clearly until someone asked.

Falling in love at first sight or more accurately, sensing the possible love connection at first sight, may be cliché; but it was a response I was given frequently enough to include it on the following list.

It was love at first:

- *Gaze into each other's eyes*
- *Touch*
- *Kiss*
- *Email – long and from the heart*
- *Touch of my face and gentle kiss*
- *Conversation*
- *Experience of seeing him completely (She didn't mean naked)*
- *Adventure*
- *Foot massage*
- *Smile – it was so warm and inviting*
- *Intimate conversation over lunch*
- *Letter*
- *Sight*

Question 6

Did you make a list of pros and cons before marrying this person?

Almost no one said "yes" to this question. Only one woman said she'd made this type of list to please a family member. All of the women said the decision to spend the rest of their lives with someone was a "feeling" decision and not a "thinking" one. They didn't have the need to make another list because their connections through feeling and knowing had confirmed the levels of intimacy they'd developed.

In an earlier chapter we talked about making a list – a list of qualities or characteristics you want in a life partner. When these standards are in place, they become an internal compass directing your choices about the type of person with whom you want to share time, energy, and love.

If you're at the point of making a long-term commitment or deciding to marry, hopefully you've already developed the foundation of intimacy for a lasting partnership. Making a list of pros and cons at this point shouldn't be necessary. If you feel that it is, put the brakes on. Evaluate the relationship honestly to assess the connection you think you feel and see. Be conscious of any red flags that may have been ignored.

Business decisions are often made through lists of pros and cons; but if you feel that way at the commitment stage of a love relationship, ask yourself what's really going on. Maybe your instincts are trying to tell you that something isn't right.

Developing and trusting your instincts is one of the best gifts you can give yourself. It's okay to take a step back and reevaluate the relationship. Direct and honest communication with yourself and your potential partner may resolve any ambiguity. That doesn't mean you can talk yourself in or out of your feelings. Rather, finding the truth will bring the clarity you need. Knowing the truth about your feelings and your partner will free you from angst over your decision – better than any list making exercise.

Question 7

What characteristics attracted you most to your spouse?

I asked the interviewees to look at the list below and circle the top five characteristics that first attracted them to their partners. I then asked them to rank their choices in order of importance.

The answers during this part of the interview were enlightening. The results, when averaged and weighted by rank order, validated some of my opinions and experiences. One result surprised me. If you're currently in a relationship, consider answering this question for yourself before looking at the survey results below.

Financial Status	*Appearance*	*Integrity*	*Job*
Social Skills	*Compatibility*	*Trust*	*Car*
Sexual Connection	*Spirituality*	*Values*	*Health*
Religion	*Family*	*House*	*Strength*
Grace	*Smell*	*Other*	

Trust: By far this was the most prevalent choice. Over half (56%) chose this quality first. 73% percent put trust in their top five. Now that you've read some of their stories, you may not be surprised at the result. My surprise was the large percentage of women who selected trust as their number one quality.

Appearance: I didn't expect women to rank appearance so high on their list -maybe the top five. It was the second most prevalent choice coming in at fifty percent. Over half of the women who selected appearance chose it as their number one attraction. This result dovetails with formal research that demonstrates the criticality of physical attractiveness. Looks count, but in the sense that partners find each other physically attractive – not by other's standards.

Integrity: This finding probably does not surprise anyone. Integrity was the third most popular choice among the top five. Of the women who chose integrity, one quarter of them selected it as their number one. Although trust and integrity are not the same thing, they are closely related. As a result, some women felt they had this one covered when they selected trust. It's clear that honesty and integrity are vital and necessary components for a happy, satisfying relationship. When integrity was compromised in these women's lives, the result was a huge crack in the foundation of the partnership. For some, the relationship didn't crumble right away, but eventually, it could not survive a breach of integrity.

Compatibility: Actually, no one chose compatibility as their number one choice. However, this characteristic received enough votes to rank in the top five. This choice is important in the development of harmony between every couple. Harmony was the essential component in the definition of the word, compatibility. Disharmony brought dissonance; and as in a musical composition, there is only so much dissonance we want to listen to before the piece loses its luster. The women you've met here valued spending time together engaged in activities from the routine, mundane to the opposite end of the spectrum. High levels of compatibility are needed for this to occur. The value placed on this quality went beyond shared activities to include finances, temperaments, and social interactions.

Sexual Connection: Coming in at number five, sexual connection was absolutely important to women of all ages, regardless of how long they had been together. It was number one for only a few. Most ranked it somewhere between three and five. One of the messages from this finding is that sexual connection does not eclipse trust, appearance, integrity, or compatibility. Sexual connection enhances the other characteristics as evidenced by its ranking in the top five for women who'd been with their partners from two years to over thirty-five years.

Values: Values came in sixth place closely behind sexual connection. This may be because of the close link between values, trust and integrity.

Spirituality, Strength, Social Skills, Grace, Family, and ***Health*** received very few votes in comparison. ***Smell*** received one vote as did ***Financial Status***.

The woman who chose financial status as number five in her top five explained that she did so after being taken advantage of by many men in her life. Marian spent quite a sum of her own money supporting men she referred to as "broke losers." Her answer was not about a partner having a specific bank account balance, but it was a realization of the significant imbalance in this area of her previous relationships.

There were zero votes for ***House, Job,*** or ***Religion***.

The only write-in choice was **Sense of Humor.** Perhaps that should have been on the list; nevertheless, it received a small percentage of votes.

Some research ranks ***Sense of Humor*** above ***Sexual Satisfaction***. Not so from the women taking this survey – the women who have the love of their lives.

Although this research was not scientifically conducted, I loved doing it. The findings are interesting and revealing. These results reflect the actual experiences and thoughts of the women in this book. If these women have what you desire for your life, consider what this research might mean in the context of your love relationship.

My parting gift to you is an affirmation to use as an example to write your own. Words spoken from the heart to the *Universe* are powerful sources of co-creation.

I hope you have enjoyed this book and were inspired by the ***It's All About You Love Coaching Program*** as well.

Namaste!

Affirmation

Today I celebrate the beauty, peace,
and happiness I know is mine;

The smile on my face reflects the joy in my heart;

I embrace my wholeness in gratitude
for all that I have and all that I am becoming;

I welcome into my life the manifestation of my heart's desire
for the perfect, loving and supportive partner for me;

I walk confidently through my day,
assured that I am loved, loving, and lovable;

Life's abundance flows to and
through me for my highest good;

I am encircled in love now and always;

I listen to the voice within receiving
all the guidance I require;

I send my heart's desires into the Universe,
prepared to accept the gift of pure and genuine love;

And So It Is!

Beyond the Book

While I've given you many of the basic steps in my ***Love Coaching Program – It's All About You***, there are limitations on how much can be shared in the context of the book. The complete ***Love Coaching Program*** includes additional materials, tools, steps and exercises based on my experience and expertise. Two of the tools I use in this program to facilitate learning and changes are NLP (neuro-linguistic programing) and EFT (Emotional Freedom Technique or Tapping). I'm a certified NLP practitioner and have studied and applied EFT for years. Both techniques are highly effective in supporting dramatic transformation for my clients.

To contact me and learn more about my full ***Love Coaching Program – It's All About You*** go to www.GaylaWick.com. You're invited to schedule a complimentary consultation and together we can determine if this program is right for you.

About The Author

Gayla Wick, transformational love coach, author, and speaker, left corporate America to coach women on how to attract their authentic love connection. Using NLP and other creative techniques, she guides clients through four types of intimacy to create deeply satisfying and sustainable love relationships. Gayla lives in Colorado with her husband, Allan.

CPSIA information can be obtained
at www.ICGtesting.com
Printed in the USA
LVHW02s1043280518
578633LV00001B/40/P

9 781504 346542